**THE GUINNESS
BOOK OF SILVER**

Congratulations on your
Silver Wedding

from,

Mike and Bernice

THE GUINNESS
BOOK OF
Silver

GEOFFREY WILLS

GUINNESS SUPERLATIVES LIMITED
2 Cecil Court, London Road, Enfield, Middlesex

Editor: Beatrice Frei
Design and Layout: Jean Whitcombe
Copyright © Geoffrey Wills and Guinness Superlatives Ltd, 1983

Published in Great Britain by
Guinness Superlatives Ltd, 2 Cecil Court, London Road,
Enfield, Middlesex

Set in Palatino
Filmset by Fakenham Photosetting Ltd, Norfolk
Printed and bound in Great Britain by William Clowes (Beccles) Ltd, Suffolk

British Library Cataloguing in Publication Data

Wills, Geoffrey
    The Guinness book of silver.
    1. Silverware, English – Collectors and
    collecting
    I. Title
    739.2'3742   NK7144

    ISBN 0–85112–222–1

Contents

Late sixteenth-century German pottery
jug with English silver-gilt mounts, 1594.
Height 27 cm. *Christie's*

Introduction

This survey of silver wares is concentrated on those made in the British Isles between 1660 and 1900. The former date marks the time when silver generally became available to others than the Church and the very wealthy. The metal is followed from the mine to the table, sideboard or cabinet, with due attention paid to the diligent supervision of the Goldsmiths' Company. It is a supervision that has ensured for many centuries a world-wide respect for English silver and its makers; one that will continue to be accorded to it far into the future.

Some of the examples illustrated are exhibited in museums, while many of them have been sold by auction in recent years; the latter demonstrating that a collector need not despair of finding first-class pieces.

Thanks are due to those who have supplied photographs for reproduction and whose names are appended in each instance. The line-drawings of marks are by Roger Penhallurick.

Geoffrey Wills

The Significance of Silver

In his Dictionary, first published in 1755, Samuel Johnson gave three meanings for the word Silver: it is 'a hard and white metal, next in weight to gold'; it is 'anything of soft splendour'; and it describes 'money made of silver'. Two centuries later, these remain acceptable definitions and go some way towards explaining why mankind has esteemed the metal since prehistoric times. In addition, there are tangible reasons for its wide popularity. Not least is its attractive appearance: pure white in colour with a noteworthy metallic lustre. On practical grounds it stands second to gold as the most malleable and ductile of metals: a single gramme of silver can be drawn out into a length of wire measuring 180 m, and silver leaf can be beaten to a thickness of 0.00025 millimetres.

Silver was known to the Romans as *argentum*, deriving from this word its chemical symbol *Ag*. The metal exists in minute quantities in sea-water and on land, where it occurs as an amalgam with mercury as well as alloyed with other metals. It is found also in a pure form, when it is termed 'native silver', but in the main it is extracted from sulphides of which it forms a constituent. These latter ores usually yield lead or copper, and in the past any silver recovered was a valuable bonus. The ore was treated by crushing and then roasting it with chemicals or mixing it with mercury, in the latter instance driving off the mercury with heat and recovering it for further use. The silver was additionally treated to remove remaining impurities, so far as that was possible according to knowledge at the time, but there were almost invariably traces of copper that defied removal.

From the sixteenth to the nineteenth century the majority of the world's silver came from Mexico, which remained the most prolific source until overtaken by the United States. Good supplies were also obtained further to the south in the same continent, notably in Peru and Bolivia. The discovery of large silver deposits in Australia and the States significantly increased world production. In the latter country, in the state of Nevada, the famous Comstock lode was found in 1859, leading to an annual output over the years 1862–8 averaging $11 000 000. In 1873 a further and even richer source was located in the area, the Great Bonanza mine, yielding enormous fortunes to John W. Mackay, an Irish-born immigrant, and his partners. Production from the Comstock and other mines in Nevada and elsewhere in the country was 116 000 oz in 1860, rising to 57 000 000 oz by 1900.

In Australia the equally-fabulous Broken Hill mines in New South Wales, discovered in 1883, added their quota to world output. From a comparatively insignificant 36 000 oz in 1885, the figure rose to

7 700 000 oz in 1890. In comparison with those figures and those for America the total European output in 1900 was 17 000 000 oz, and overall world output in the same year amounted to 180 000 000 oz. This invites a vision of many thousands of three-piece teasets and so forth, but in fact only a small proportion of the metal reached the skilful hands of silversmiths; most of it was used in manufacturing processes, including growing quantities in photographic plates, films and paper.

As regards Europe, silver was mined in Germany from the tenth century onwards and Spanish mines were active until the fifteenth century, when the metal began to be imported in quantity from the country's South American possessions. Only comparatively small amounts were produced in England, mainly in the west and south-west of the country. In 1602, Richard Carew noted in his *Survey of Cornwall*:

> 'Neither hath nature denyed Silver to Cornwall, though Cicero excluded the same out of all Britaine: and if we may beleeve our Chroniclers reports, who ground themselves upon authenticall Records, king Edward the first, and king Edward the third, reaped some good benefit thereof.'

There are occasional mentions of Cornish silver during later periods, including a paragraph printed in the *Gentleman's Magazine* of March 1812:

> 'Benjamin Tucker, esq. surveyor-general of the Duchy of Cornwall, presented to the Prince Regent an elegant snuff-box, made of silver extracted from Wheal Duchy silver mine, in the manor of Calstock, parcel of the Duchy of Cornwall, now working under the auspices of his Royal Highness.'

Although situated in the area of the riverside village of Calstock, the mine in question was a few miles away at Harrowbarrow, where its remains are still visible. In recent years the local inn was briefly re-named 'The Silver Wheal' (wheal meaning mine) before reverting to its original title of 'The Carpenters' Arms'.

The adjoining county of Devon proved more profitable and there, too, the thirteenth and fourteenth centuries saw considerable activity. The mines were at first managed at the royal expense, but were later leased to the highest bidder or granted to favoured subjects for stated periods. The most productive in the county were at Bere Alston and Bere Ferrers, near Tavistock and across the river Tamar from Calstock, and in the north at Combe Martin. The last-named was worked at intervals with varying success during five hundred years, finally being abandoned in 1875; when, despite evidence of so much human burrowing the little seaside village became a popular holiday resort. During the reign of Elizabeth I the mines at Combe Martin came into the hands of a skilled engineer of the day, Sir Bevis Bulmer. In 1593 he presented a 'rich and fair cup' to William, Earl of Bath, and another complete with cover and weighing a total of 137 oz, to the Lord Mayor of London, both of the cups engraved with verses extolling Bulmer's share in gaining the ore from which they had been made.

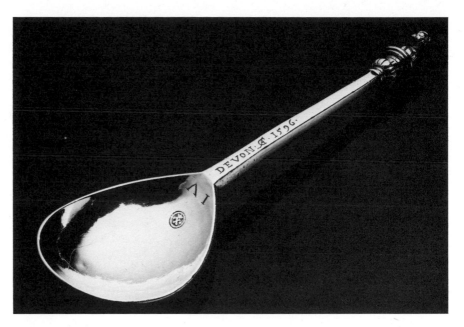

Spoon by John Edis, Exeter, *c.* 1596.
Length 18 cm. *Royal Albert Memorial
Museum, Exeter.* The terminal is the
figure of a squirrel from the crest of the
Gilbert family of Compton, Devon, and it
is engraved with the initials of Adrian
Gilbert; he is known to have had an
interest in the Combe Martin silver
mines, so it is not unlikely that the spoon
is made of metal from that source

Daniel Lysons published a history of Devonshire in 1822, remarking that the mines at Bere Alston and Bere Ferrers were notable for the length of time during which they had been worked, as well as for the proportion of silver they contained: 'the silver in each ton of lead being from 80 ounces to 120'. He added that one or other of the mines (probably Bere Alston, but Lysons himself seemed uncertain) yielded 6500 oz in 1784 and 1785. In 1809 there was a further re-opening of Bere Alston mine, capital for the purpose being raised by the issue of 3000 shares at £100 each. At one period 6000 oz of silver were produced in the course of six weeks, but this pace did not endure and the venture ended.

Further north, in Wales, the Gadlys lead mines, near Aberdare in mid-Glamorgan, were stated to have produced as much as 430 604 oz of silver between 1704 and 1744, about 10 000 oz per annum. A jug in the National Museum of Wales that dates from *c.* 1710 was made from metal mined at Bwlch Yr Eskchir, and is inscribed to that effect.

The supply of home-produced silver was inadequate to satisfy demand, so it was necessary to obtain the balance from elsewhere. Imports from other countries were augmented whenever possible by the ships of the Navy and by privateers, whose main targets in 1730–50 were Spanish and Portuguese vessels returning laden from South America. Now forbidden by international law, the privateer was a privately-owned armed craft commissioned by the Government to act as a man-o-war. When the Navy and the legalised pirates returned to port after a successful sortie they were likely to be received with acclamation. In November 1739 the *Gentleman's Magazine* reported:

'Several tons of Silver, taken out of the St. Joseph a Caracca Ship, were brought from Portsmouth, guarded by a Troop of Horse, with the King's Trumpets and Drums playing before them, and lodged in the Bank of England.'

A month earlier there had also been a spectacular haul:

> '. . . Admiral Haddock, besides lesser Prizes, has intercepted two rich Ships . . . having on Board 2,000,000 Pieces of Eight, one of which of 800 Tun is arrived at Spithead worth above £150,000 with the crew, being 76 Spaniards.'

It should be mentioned that we were then on the brink of war with Spain.

Perhaps the richest of such welcome cargoes was taken in 1743 when Commodore (later Admiral) Anson of the Royal Navy was cruising off Manila in search of the Spanish treasure ship making its annual voyage from Acapulco to Manila. After a month of fruitless sailing he came upon the galleon, the *Nuestra Señora del Caba Donga*; a vessel much superior in size, armament and number of crew to his own *Centurion*. Nevertheless, during an engagement of 90 minutes the Spaniard had his masts and rigging shot to pieces, sustained 150 shots through her hull and suffered 58 killed and 83 wounded out of her complement of 550. Anson suffered only two men killed and 15 wounded, and a mere 15 shots pierced the *Centurion*'s hull. He was then faced with the task of bringing home the booty, which comprised not only his recent capture but other amounts taken during the four-year voyage. The ship reached Portsmouth in June 1744, a press paragraph stating:

> 'The Cargo which Commodore Anson has brought home with him is as follows, viz. 2,600,000 Pieces of Eight, 150,000 Ounces of Plate, 10 Bars of Gold, and a large Quantity of Gold and Silver Dust; in the whole to the Amount of £1,250,000 Sterling.'

It is not surprising to learn, therefore, that 32 wagons were required to move such an abundance through the streets of London to the Tower. The convoy was guarded by the crew preceded by the ship's officers with drawn swords, and there was music and, not least, the colours of Anson's squadron and of the Spaniard.

So much for the basic material and whence it came, attention must turn now to what was done with it over the centuries. Understandably, knowledge of silverware made and used in pre-Tudor times is scanty. It relies largely on such mentions as were made at the time in documents, supported by examples that have survived the passage of the years; some of them having been found in tombs and others preserved by mere chance. From them it is neither possible to gauge the total quantity available at any one period, nor to know just how wide a range of articles was made, because many have doubtless vanished without trace. Also, there is no way of telling what proportion of their kind the survivors represent.

The greatest repositories of silver prior to the sixteenth century were cathedrals, churches and other ecclesiastical establishments which, in the course of time, had been the recipients of gifts great and small from pious benefactors. The treasuries of many of the larger places sheltered more than they could use or would normally display, those in charge ignoring the Bible's injunction: 'lay not up for yourselves treasures upon earth . . .'.

In 1535 the Law of Supremacy was passed, confirming the independence of the Church of England, terminating the connection with Rome and stating that the King was 'the only supreme head in earth of the Church of England'. Shortly afterwards the reigning monarch, Henry VIII, dissolved the various religious orders, demolishing their buildings and annexing the contents, and the principal shrines were plundered. It is perhaps arguable whether this was done because they had ceased to exist for the common good of the populace, or if Henry simply coveted their possessions. Whatever the reason, the result was, as G. M. Trevelyan put it: '5,000 monks, 1,600 friars and 2,000 nuns were pensioned off and sent out into the world'. Their wealth in jewels and plate, the latter conjecturally estimated to amount to 290 000 oz, being mostly destroyed and converted into coinage.

One feature of the reformed Church was the introduction of a new form of sacramental service, a move that led to the replacement of the Romish chalice by the Protestant communion cup. The earliest surviving example of such a cup is one at St Lawrence Jewry, London, hall-marked 1548, and there are a few others remaining from shortly after that date, but it was not until the reign of Elizabeth I that there was compulsion for the clergy to obtain communion cups.

The cups and patens were often locally made, the churchwardens supplying a surplus or out-dated chalice or some other piece of plate for the purpose. On at least one occasion there remained a surplus of metal, and the Maidstone silversmith to whom the officers at Smarden, Kent, sent their chalice returned to them a new cup and the sum of 7s 4d in addition. Sometimes an early flat paten was reshaped into one of the new domed type, leaving it with tell-tale traces of the original engraving.

Church plate has not been free from similar interference in more modern times, but it has been for different reasons. Nineteenth-century reformers advocated changes in ritual as well as in style: the once-derided 'barbarous' Gothic was reinstated in place of a classical simplicity that had been accepted for so long. In the case of plate, the vestry might now decide that an article was too out of fashion, or too worn, to be commendable in the light of contemporary thinking, and as a result might be exchanged for something modern. Alternatively, it might be sent away for re-making. For example, at St Thomas the Martyr, Salisbury, two chalices with patens and a flagon were treated in that manner, the replacements being inscribed to the effect that they had been re-cast from earlier gifts. The names of the original donors and dates were given, the latter ranging from 1597 to 1689; 'all these pieces are of silver gilt and bear the hall-mark of 1867', wrote J. E. Nightingale.

Although so much of the existing plate in the past was in the possession of the Church, it was also owned and appreciated by the wealthier inhabitants of the country. With a store of plate to hand, a man was never poor and could speedily convert all or some into cash or goods. This was essential in the days before banks existed, when the goldsmith (who also handled silver despite his name) combined the roles of supplier of finished goods and that of provider of banking services.

Describing the Elizabethan England in which he lived, William

Harrison wrote of the noblemen's houses in which it was common to see 'rich hangings of tapestry, silver vessel, so much other plate as may furnish sundry cupboards to the sum oftentimes of a thousand or two thousand pounds at the least . . .'. The better-off citizen, he continued, would possess plate valued at between five hundred and a thousand pounds, but just as those classes had become enriched in comparison with their predecessors so, at the time he wrote, 'inferior artificers and many farmers . . . have . . . learned also to garnish their cupboards with plate'. Harrison did not reproach them for this, but pointed out that it demonstrated the comfortable state of the country in the 1580s and, to quote words used on a later occasion, that the inhabitants had 'never had it so good'.

The cupboard, court cupboard or sideboard, was made with shelves specifically for the display of plate, and more was to be seen on the dining table. Foremost was a standing salt holding a token quantity of the condiment, but of which the principal purpose was to divide the host and diners of equal importance from lesser mortals; the first sat 'above the salt' and the remainder below it. Also, there would be silver and gilt vessels and dishes, candlesticks and spoons, while between the courses a servant would pour water from a silver ewer into a bowl so that fingers could be cleaned after handling sticky and greasy food.

Another reason for its possession was that it was decorative as well as valuable: a sideboard decked with large pieces in the form of cups and dishes, whether silver or silver-gilt, could not fail to impress on a visitor the importance of an occasion and the prestige of the host. As with the churches, the majority of what existed in homes of the period has vanished except for written descriptions and occasional depictions in illuminations, woodcuts and engravings. However, these are sufficient in number and clarity to give a general idea of many of the riches that have disappeared forever. Comparable in scope to the ravages of time were the great losses that took place at a later date, in the seventeenth century, when the rival armies engaged in the Civil War seized or 'borrowed' every item of silver on which they could lay their hands. Melted and converted into coinage, the booty was used for the essential requirements of the time, for buying arms, ammunition and food and, not least, for paying the troops. The wholesale looting, for that word is not too strong to describe what occurred in so many instances, took place up and down the country almost everywhere that there was military activity.

A further use for silver at that date and later was to enhance the appearance of a rarity, or to convert such an object from being merely decorative into one with a function. Thus, many of the earliest examples of Chinese porcelain brought to England in the sixteenth century were carefully fitted with bases, rims and handles of the metal, which had a further effect of stressing their importance and helping to preserve them intact over the years. As well as man-made specimens of pottery, porcelain, glass and other materials, natural curiosities were treated in the same manner. Ostrich eggs, seashells, rare hardstones and coconut shells were among the many things that were transformed into goblets, tank-

Standing salt and cover, maker's mark R M with pellets below, 1581. Silver-gilt, height 27.9 cm. *Christie's.* The cover is surmounted by a soldier holding a spear

Ewer, mounts with maker's mark E I in a shaped shield, *c.* 1610. Height 28 cm. *Christie's.* It is made from a Chinese porcelain vessel (*kendi*) of the Wanli period (1573–1619) painted in blue under the glaze and mounted in silver when it reached England

ards and so forth to make them usable; although it may be thought that in many instances they served as decoration or as 'collector's pieces', rather than as drinking vessels. Into that category probably fell an item listed in an inventory taken in 1741: 'One Coal Tankard with a Silver Cover and handle and two Body ringes of Silver'; which would have been made from a lump of Cannel coal, a bituminous type of coal that can be worked and polished so that it resembles jet. In more modern times, Australian silversmiths have mounted the eggs of the emu, a native of the country and a source of appropriate souvenirs.

When Charles II landed at Dover on 25 May 1660 and was crowned at Westminster in the following April, he did more than re-establish the monarchy in a country that had suffered the dullness of Cromwellian rule. Charles had been forced to live in exile on the Continent since fleeing the country in 1646, apart from a brief and unsuccessful visit to Scotland in 1650–51 to regain his crown, and had imbibed foreign ideas and habits. These were reinforced when in 1662 he married Catherine of Braganza, daughter of the King of Portugal. There had been few signs of luxury during the years of Puritan domination, so that when Charles ascended the throne the nation was suddenly set free from a rigid restraint.

Within a couple of weeks of the future King's return the issue of a proclamation resulted in the return of some of the paintings, silver and other valuables that had been pillaged earlier from the Palace of Whitehall. It was some years, however, before John Evelyn could record a positive return to times past; in August 1667 he noted, 'Now did his Majestie againe dine in the Presence, in antient State, with Musique & all the Court ceremonies, which had been interrupted since the late warr'.

Charles was no less lavish with his purse than with his favours and the ladies of the Court lacked no encouragement to pursue a path of extravagance, many of the nobles following suit according to

Silver-mounted iron fire-pan, *c.* 1675.
*Ham House (Victoria and
Albert Museum)*

their wealth and tastes. The actress Nell Gwynn, much admired by
Samuel Pepys and referred to by him as 'pretty witty Nell', was the
recipient in 1674 of a silver bedstead. This was doubtless constructed
of wood and iron covered with sheet silver, embossed and
engraved, and it cost just over £900. This sum probably did not
include the 'furniture', comprising curtains and other hangings
which normally exceeded the value of the actual bed, so the total
figure would have been considerably higher. The bed, which some
might dub a mis-application of the silversmith's art, vanished long
ago into the melting-pot.

The milieu of the French-born Louise de Keroualle, ennobled as
Duchess of Portsmouth and another favourite of Charles, was
visited and commented on by John Evelyn. The entry in his diary for
4 October 1683 records the people and their background that met his
gaze at Whitehall:

'Following his Majestie this morning through the Gallerie [I] went
(with the few who attended him) into the Duchesse of Ports-
mouths dressing roome, within her bed-chamber, where she was
in her morning loose garment, her maides Combing her, newly
out of her bed: his Majestie & the Gallants standing about her: but
that which ingag'd my curiositie, was the rich & splendid furniture of this woman's Appartment, now twice or thrice, puld
downe, & rebuilt, to satisfie her prodigal & expensive pleasures,
whilst her Majestie dos not exceede, some gentlemens Ladies
furniture & accomodation: Here I saw the new fabrique of *French
Tapissry* ... Then for *Japon* [lacquer] *Cabinets, Skreenes, Pendule*
Clocks, huge *Vasàs* of wrought plate, *Tables, Stands, Chimny furniture, Sconces, branches, Braseras* [wall-lights, chandeliers and
braziers] &c they were all of massive silver, & without number . . .'

There still survive a few examples of such prodigality. Ham
House, near Richmond, retains silver-mounted chimney-furniture

in more than one of its rooms: pairs of andirons, sets of tongs, shovel, brush and bellows and silver-mounted firepan, the latter probably for burning charcoal. The bedroom named The Volury had 'one fire pan done with silver' according to an inventory taken in 1677, but today only three leaf-pattern silver feet survive to confirm the written record.

Rooms in several other houses were furnished like that of the Duchess of Portsmouth, each with a suite comprising a table placed below a hanging looking-glass and flanked by tall candlestands. Celia Fiennes, who visited many of the important houses in England during the reign of William and Mary, called at the Earl of Chesterfield's mansion, Bretby Hall, Derbyshire. She noted that one of the apartments she was shown was a bedroom that had been known formerly as The Silver Room, having contained 'stands, table and fire utensils' of the metal. This and the other plate in the house had been sold, Celia Fiennes wrote, because of the Earl's objection to paying the tax on silver.

The fashion for the suites of table, looking-glass and candlestands, as well as for other pieces of furniture made of silver, was neither confined to nor originated in England. The fashion came from across the Channel where, in France for instance, the enormous Grande Galerie and other rooms at Versailles had furnishings of silver to provide a spectacular background for the Court of Louis XIV.

Royal gifts were often of an equally ostentatious nature. In May 1667 Samuel Pepys noted that he had seen at the premises of the banker/goldsmith Sir Robert Vyner 'two or three great silver flagons, made with inscriptions as gifts of the King to such and such persons of quality as did stay in town the late great plague, for the keeping things in order in the town'. The diarist also recorded occasions on which he gave or received gifts of plate in return for favours performed or anticipated. There is no shortage of specimens of all dates bearing inscriptions denoting that they had changed hands under similar circumstances. Among interesting examples are a number of vases that were the gift of Lloyds to captains of vessels involved in naval actions in the early 1800s.

In the same category were the silver dishes presented annually to the Lord Mayor of London by the congregation of Bevis Marks synagogue in the City. In 1719 this took the form of a four-handled dish, repoussé and chased centrally with a tent guarded by a man with a banner bearing the lion of Judah and holding a spear. Above the tent was the inscription 'The Arms of the Tribe of Judah Given them by the Lord'. The dishes were given from 1679 until the mid-eighteenth century and then a cup was substituted until 1778, when the custom ceased on account of its cost.

Public esteem of silver was also to be witnessed, rather unexpectedly, on the streets in the annual frolics of the London milkmaids. This custom began at some time towards the close of the seventeenth century and continued probably for a hundred years, beginning on May Day, 1 May, and lasting about a week. The girls, who walked the streets of London daily supplying milk from pails borne on their heads, went from street to street in search of gifts of money.

They must have been a familiar and popular sight, and they feature in the backgrounds of quite a number of topographical paintings. A good description of the entertainment provided by the milkmaids, many of whom were Irish immigrants, was given by J. T. Smith in *A Book for a Rainy Day*, published in 1845. It contained personal reminiscences covering the preceding 60 years, and under the heading 1771 Smith wrote:

> 'The gaiety of the merry month of May was to me most delightful; my feet, though I knew nothing of the positions, kept pace with those of the blooming milkmaids, who danced round their garlands of massive plate, hired from the silversmiths to the amount of several hundreds of pounds, for the purpose of placing round an obelisk, covered with silk fixed upon a chairman's horse. The most showy flowers of the season were arranged so as to fill up the openings between the dishes, plates, butter-boats, cream-jugs, and tankards. This obelisk was carried by two chairmen in gold-laced hats . . . but what crowned the whole display was a magnificent silver tea-urn which surmounted the obelisk, the stand of which was profusely decorated with scarlet tulips.'

A painting of one of these May Day scenes by Francis Hayman

Dish by Robert Hill, 1719. Width 61 cm. *Christie's.* Presented to the Lord Mayor of London, Sir George Thorold, in 1719 by the congregation of the Bevis Marks Synagogue

May Day by Francis Hayman (1708–76).
Victoria and Albert Museum. Painted to
decorate a box at Vauxhall Gardens

once decorated a box at Vauxhall Gardens, the fashionable
pleasure-resort close to the Thames from the 1660s until final closure
in 1859. From that date, Hayman's picture vanished, but was re-
discovered in the present century and can now be seen in the
Victoria and Albert Museum. An earlier engraving, dating to *c.* 1700,
shows a milkmaid dancing while bearing on her head a small pile of
silver decked with flowers, and as was the case with her later sister
the music was provided by a fiddler.

The prestige accorded to silver has been reflected in its continuing comparatively high money value and the care taken to safeguard it. The Royal possessions of the metal, no less than those of other owners, were a precious asset as well as an important symbol and were treated with due consequence. This is exemplified by the existence of the Royal Jewel House; from its careful records can be gleaned much about the types of articles that were in being and about the effects of historical events. An inventory of the contents of

the Jewel House was taken in 1574, during the reign of Elizabeth I;
two copies of the document are extant and were edited and printed
in 1955.

The Jewel House was the repository of the Crown Jewels, using
that term in a wide sense to embrace not only, as now, the regalia,
but the many jewels and articles of gold and silver in the ownership
of the monarch. They were held in safe custody so as to be readily
available when required: the regalia for occasions of State, and the
remainder to furnish the palaces with whatever was required for
display and for the table. In addition, the Jewel House could furnish
objects suitable to serve as gifts to favoured citizens and foreign
visitors, such as ambassadors, potentates and distinguished overseas personages in return for the gifts traditionally borne by them
and ceremonially presented. The sovereign's personal jewellery
was kept separately in the care of a Gentleman or a Gentlewoman
(in the case of the Queen) of the Privy Chamber.

The numerous items kept in the Jewel House were carefully listed,
checked and re-checked and comprised the many acquisitions of
Henry VIII, both by way of seizure and purchased with money
realised by the former, together with gifts; which might often be
described more accurately as bribes or extortions from his loyal
subjects. To these were added Edward VI's exaction from the
Church of further treasures; this time of a lesser amount estimated at
about 200 000 oz. The sovereign might be the recipient of gifts at any
time but they were especially prevalent on New Year's Day, when
all who sought or had received favours attended Court and marked
their presence by making an offering. The higher the status of the
donor, the more imposing was the gift, which would be matched by
one in return.

Such ritual presents were possibly given in person by the
monarch to a favoured subject, but in 1661 Pepys had been deputed,
along with Henry Moore who was a member of the household of the
Earl of Sandwich, to select a suitable Royal gift for his patron the
Earl. At the same time, he recorded how the matter was strictly
regulated:

'4 January ... dined at Home, and Mr. Moore with me – with
whom I had been early this morning at White-hall at the Jewell-
Office, to choose of a piece of gilt plate for my Lord in returne of
his offering to the King (which it seems is usuall at this time of the
year, and an Earle gives 20 pieces in gold in a purse to the King); I
chose a gilt tankard weighing 31 ounces and a half, and he is
allowed 30; so I paid 12s for the ounce and a half over what he is to
have. But strange it was for me to see what a company of small
Fees I was called upon by a great many to pay there; which I
perceive is the manner that courtiers do get their estates.'

The Royal collection suffered its first large-scale depletion in 1600,
when the Queen ordered the disposal of 300 items designated 'useless', or in modern words 'surplus to requirements'. Her successor,
James I, early in his reign concluded a treaty with Philip III of Spain
which was signed in London in August 1604. To mark the occasion,
the Constable of Castile and Leon and his fellow-commissioners

were presented with gold vessels weighing a total of 290 oz and with 29 000 oz of gilt plate, with which they returned to Spain well-satisfied, one imagines, leaving large spaces on the shelves of the Jewel House. The booty included a ewer and basin that had been made in about 1536 especially for Henry VIII's wife, Jane Seymour, and had quite possibly been designed by Holbein. Also they took 'The Royal Gold Cup of the Kings of France and England', made of gold with decoration in coloured enamel. It had been made in France in about 1380, coming to this country some fifty years later where it was duly owned by Henry VI, remaining in the care of the Jewel House under successive sovereigns until removed by order of James. Because it stayed in this country for so long and because of its historical significance, it might be considered as having acquired English nationality despite the general acceptance of its cross-Channel origin. The cup came on the market in 1883, and was eventually bought by the British Museum where it now rests, it may be hoped, for all time.

In 1620 James I disposed of more 'useless' articles and his son, Charles I, continued to do the same; both of them cast a wide net in selecting what should go, the intrinsic value of the metal usually being elevated above utility. Then came the Civil War, with the Parliamentarians, once in power, wasting no time in seizing what remained in the Jewel House, converting it into coin at the Mint so that a minimum reached the hands of sinful goldsmiths. According to Puritan thinking they would have re-fashioned the metal into what were considered to be wicked vanities.

Nearly two centuries later there came a further loss of Royal silver. This was in 1808 when the Prince of Wales (later Prince Regent) was making arrangements for his estranged wife, Caroline, to have apartments of her own in Kensington Palace. The Prince was, as always, very short of money if not penniless, and proposed that some of the items in the care of the Jewel House, each of which was 'neither available for service in its present form nor valuable for its antiquity or workmanship', should be sold. The consent of the ailing

Dinner service by Thomas Heming and other makers, various dates. *Christie's.* The service was issued by the Jewel House to Sir John Cust, elected Speaker of the House of Commons in 1761 and 1768; each piece is engraved with the Royal arms of George III

George III, whose current state of health was the reason for the Regency, was obtained for this to be carried out, and the articles were disposed of. The buyers were the Royal goldsmiths, Rundell, Bridge and Rundell, who paid the bare value of the metal. Doubtless it was assumed by the King and his advisers that the objects would go to the melting-pot, but this was not done and the firm sold them more profitably to some of their wealthy clients. In the course of time many of the articles have been recognised as having passed into the possession of prominent connoisseurs of the day.

Although many of the important treasures in the Jewel House had been disposed of by the close of the seventeenth century, it continued to function thereafter in a way that earned it a further mention in the history of silver. One of its later tasks was to equip ambassadors and others with plate to support their position as representatives abroad of their monarch. To this end, the Jewel House granted loans of tableware, which could embrace dishes, tureens, etc, and eating-implements as well as candlesticks, to ambassadors about to travel abroad and to a number of statesmen who included the Speaker of the House of Commons. To proclaim both the status of the borrower and the ownership of the items, each was engraved boldly with the Royal coat of arms and usually also with the Royal initials.

The individual concerned was required to give his signature for whatever was issued to him, but despite this precaution there were many occasions when some or all of the items were not returned. Sometimes this took place when an ambassador, for one reason or another, overspent his allowance for entertaining and other expenses, and it would then be expedient to settle the outstanding balance by permitting retention of the corresponding value in plate. In time, however, it became customary for the loans to be looked on as outright gifts and perquisites of office with no question of their surrender to the Jewel House. Between 1685 and 1715 more than forty instances of this practice were known to have occurred, involving some 68 000 oz of silver and 5000 oz of silver-gilt: no small amount, even if the loss to the country was spread over a period of thirty years.

By the early nineteenth century the state of affairs had grown worse, with recipients being allowed cash instead of silverware. In 1815 George Tierney, member of Parliament for Appleby, a sharp critic of the Government, raised the matter in the House.

'He believed that, instead of the usual allowance of plate, some of the Ambassadors took money. A Mr. William Hill, and Mr. A'Court, who were only envoys, had £3500 for plate, as if they had been Ambassadors.'

This seems to have been the beginning of the end, and in due course the giving of what were in effect costly gifts to the monarch's representatives terminated. Instead, the embassies were each provided with plate that was a part of the furnishing, like the tables and chairs and so forth, which passed from each occupant to his successor. In 1839 the comparable gift to the Speaker also ceased to be made.

The Regulation of the Craft

Pure silver is too soft to withstand normal use, but the addition to it of a small amount of copper leaves its appearance unchanged and at the same time transforms it into a durable material. However, the goldsmith (or silversmith, the two terms being interchangeable) was only human, and there were craftsmen who were less than honest in defrauding the public by adulterating the silver with overmuch base metal. This was possible because as much as 50 per cent of copper can be added without visible effect. With protection of gold and silver currency in mind, the authorities have always kept a wary eye on the activities of those concerned with the metals.

Two principal methods have been employed to determine the amount of alloy present in a silver article: touching and weighing. The first-named involves touching (or rubbing) the metal with a piece of slate-like stone, basanite, and comparing the colour of the silver taken up by the stone with the colour of a rubbing of known fineness. Experience is necessary in making the comparison, and the method is more effective for assaying gold than silver. Instead of the natural stone a piece of basaltes, the hard type of pottery developed by Josiah Wedgwood in 1768–9, can be employed.

Assaying by weight is the more accurate of the two, although the procedure is more complicated. When submitted for testing the partly finished object is weighed, and then small samples of metal are scraped from it; this being done carefully so as to cause minimal damage, the total amount removed being no more than 8 grains in weight for each Troy pound of the whole. The scrapings, termed the diet, are weighed, wrapped in a small sheet of lead and heated in a special porous crucible known as a cupel. The cupel is made of bone ash, a white powder that results from burning animals' bones, and in a heated furnace the lead and alloy are absorbed by the cupel to leave only the pure silver. This last is weighed, the weight being compared with that of the original scrapings to determine the quantity of base metal that had been present. A third method employing chemicals is also available.

As early as the year 1180 there was in existence a guild of goldsmiths, eager to regulate its own affairs and forestall governmental interference. There is no remaining record of its activities beyond the fact that it was then fined for having been established without the King's licence. Half a century later, in 1238, there was another occasion for Royal displeasure when Henry II, on account of frauds that had been perpetrated, ordered the Mayor and Aldermen of London to select six of the City's goldsmiths to supervise their craft. The six were chosen and duly succeeded by others so that in 1300, when Edward I was on the throne, the men who were now referred to as 'gardiens' were officially recognised.

Leopard's head, *c.* 1550

Troy weight comprises
the following:
1 pound equals 12 oz
(ounces, written oz)
1 oz equals 20 dwt
(pennyweights, written dwt)
1 dwt equals 24 grains

Lion passant guardant, *c.* 1560

The duties of the gardiens included the important one of assaying every silver article prior to its leaving the hands of the maker and being exposed for sale. If of acceptable standard it was to be stamped with the touch or impressed mark of a leopard's head. This was known as the King's mark, serving as an assurance that the article bearing it was of the required Sterling standard. It permitted a maximum of 18 dwt of copper to each 12 oz of silver, measured by the subsequently-adopted Troy weight; so-called because it was introduced from Troyes, France, in the fifteenth century to replace the ancient Tower weight of pounds, marks, shillings and pence. The general adoption of the metric system of weights and measures will involve expressing silver weights in grammes, and conversion tables for Troy to metric and metric to Troy are given at the end of this volume.

In 1327, the first year of the reign of Edward III, the London goldsmiths' guild was given its first charter setting out its accepted rules; an important document that was amended and renewed from time to time. On the same occasion it was stated that the importation was prohibited 'of any sort of money but only plate of fine silver' and export of gold and silver was banned. Further, no goldsmith 'shall keep any shop but in Chepe [Cheapside, in the City], that it may be seen that their work is good'.

A regulation of 1363 ordered each goldsmith to have a personal mark that was to be entered at the goldsmiths' Hall, so that the maker of an article could be identified readily should a complaint arise. At the same time it no doubt ensured that more care was taken not to break the law, as an offender might be brought to book with ease. Then, almost 100 years later, in 1467, the goldsmiths obtained from Edward IV a charter by which they were created a corporation under the resounding title of 'The Wardens and Commonalty of the Mystery of Goldsmiths of the City of London'.

Further regulations were introduced as the years passed, and in 1478 it was ordered that an additional mark should be stamped on each article. It was to be a letter of the alphabet to be changed annually on 19 May, the anniversary of the death of St Dunstan, the patron saint of the Goldsmiths' Company, so that the serving Warden responsible for the assay could be traced. Later, to commemorate the entry into London of Charles II on 29 May 1660, the date for changing the letter was altered to 29 May, which still obtains. The alphabetical mark unintentionally enabled later generations to date with precision the year of manufacture although, incidentally, it was not until 1851 that Octavius Morgan published the result of his pioneering investigation into the early date letters and listed them chronologically.

The alphabet in use from 1478 was one of 20 letters, from A to U or V omitting J. The style of lettering, and often the shape of the outline of the punch, was changed with each fresh start at A.

Finally, yet another mark was added to the existing three (leopard's head, maker's mark, date letter): an heraldic lion passant guardant, walking and looking to its left, which made its appearance in 1544. The lion denoted that the article bearing it was of Sterling standard, possibly reassuring the public at a time when Henry VIII was debasing the coinage. The leopard's head became the mark of the London Assay Office. From 1545 the animal was depicted wearing a crown, and from 1821 it was uncrowned. In the latter year the lion became a lion passant, with its head facing forward.

With the restoration of the monarchy in 1660 there came a big demand for silver wares to replace the quantities that had been melted during the Civil War. The silversmiths rose to the occasion, illegally using for the purpose clippings from the unmilled edges of the coinage as well as whole coins, which were acceptable for assaying as they were of the required standard. At length, in 1697 the Government acted to save what remained of the diminished currency and to halt the practice of clipping, after having made an earlier half-hearted attempt to do so.

The 1697 statute was a sweeping one, replacing Sterling standard by a new one named Britannia standard in which each Troy pound was composed of 11 oz 10 dwt of fine silver alloyed with 10 dwt of copper. Further, this new grade of silver would be marked with a lion's head erased (with a jagged edge at the neck), a figure of Britannia in place of the leopard's head and lion passant, and each maker was required to register a fresh personal mark in the form of the first two letters of his surname. For the first time silver wire and very small articles were freed from assaying and marking, and thenceforward goods made to order and not for stock, that had hitherto frequently escaped inspection because of a loosely-worded earlier Act, were to be submitted in the normal way.

The new standard became compulsory on 27 March 1697 and stayed in use until 1 June 1720, when a return to Sterling was permitted. Britannia standard and its relevant marks remained legal, and silversmiths again had to change their personal marks; on this occasion employing the initials of a forename and their surname. Also, certain minor items were listed as being exempted.

One further mark came into use on 1 December 1784: a duty mark in the shape of the sovereign's head, at first incuse, or sunken, but after May 1786 in cameo, or raised like the other marks. An excise duty on silver wares had been levied for the first time during the reign of George I, in 1720. It was at the rate of 6d (2½p) per oz on all articles that 'should or ought to be touched, assayed or marked', but it proved impossible to collect successfully and in its place dealers in plate were required to take out an annual licence. In 1784 the duty was re-imposed, but this time the authorities were taking no chances and ensured that the collection of the money was put on a sound basis.

When submitting his goods for assay a maker sent with each parcel of goods a ticket printed with his name and address and written brief particulars of the items and their weight together with the amount of duty involved. To demonstrate that this had been paid, each article was stamped with the Royal likeness. For a short period, from 1 December 1784 to 24 July 1785, there was a special mark for goods intended for export and on which the duty had been refunded. This last, the drawback mark, showed Britannia standing, not seated as on Britannia standard wares, and in the latter instance the figure was raised in cameo and that for drawback was

Leopard uncrowned and lion passant in use from 1821

Britannia in use from 1699

Lion's head erased in use from 1699

Sugar caster by Micon Melun, Exeter, 1733. Height 13.8 cm. *Royal Albert Memorial Museum, Exeter.* Micon Melun had his workshop at Falmouth, Cornwall, sending his wares to the nearest office, Exeter, for assay and marking

sunken: termed incuse. Duty on silver was abolished from 30 April 1890.

The surviving records of the Goldsmiths' Company include registers of makers' names and their individual stamps. The earlier ones, except for a copper plate bearing marks dating between 1675 and 1697 and mostly of unidentified silversmiths, were destroyed in a fire at the Assay Office. The records are in books, one series for Small Plate Workers and another for Large Plate Workers, named in allusion to the types of goods produced, commencing in April 1697. Each lists the craftsman's name and address and signature, together with an ink print from his metal punch and the date when the entry was made. Regrettably, the volume of Small Plate Workers for 24 May 1738 to 13 July 1758 and that of Large Plate Workers for 30 September 1759 to 7 March 1773 have vanished, and some of the identifications of the makers concerned are therefore uncertain. It is thought that the two books were among the records of the Company submitted for examination by a Parliamentary Committee in 1773, and while the others were returned these two remained at Westminster and perished in the fire at the House of Commons in 1834. From 1773 a single volume was started for both categories of workers, breaking them down further into spectacle-framers, gold workers, buckle-makers, hilt-makers, and watch-case makers.

In theory the powers of the London Goldsmiths extended over the whole country, but in practice they rarely exercised authority outside the capital. Silversmithing was not confined to London, as there are mentions of craftsmen active in the thirteenth century at Chester and Norwich and a hundred years later at York and Exeter. A statute of 1423 re-enacted the provisions of earlier regulations, appointing 'York, Newcastle-upon-Tine, Lincoln, Norwich, Bristow [Bristol], Salisbury and Coventry to have divers touches' and each to be under the control of the 'mayors, Bailiffs, or Governors of the said towns'. In addition there were silversmiths at Chester who were omitted from the foregoing list, probably because they were under the jurisdiction of the Earl of Chester.

Local investigations have revealed that there were also numerous small guilds that flourished at various dates in minor towns. Their total is occasionally increased, but even when documentary evidence of their existence is uncovered this cannot always be confirmed by actual specimens. Sotheby's catalogue of the H. D. Ellis collection of spoons, prepared in 1935 by the late Commander G. E. P. How, describes and illustrates a highly interesting variety of spoons and their marks with arguments for and against the attributions, some of which had already been published by Jackson. Included in the Ellis collection were marked spoons from most of the towns listed above, and many others ascribed to places in different parts of the country such as Beccles, Bridgwater, Bury St Edmunds, Canterbury, Chelmsford, Coggeshall, Colchester, Gloucester, Ilminster, Ipswich, King's Lynn, Plymouth, Reading, Romsey, Shaftesbury, Sherborne, Southampton, Sudbury, Taunton, Tavistock and Truro.

There would have been a number of reasons for such a proliferation of towns, each with its individual stamp. Not least was the risk in transporting goods to the bigger centres over poor roads, with the possibility of robbery or damage. There was also account to be taken of local pride in craftsmanship and a probable mistrust of rivals.

In 1667 the reputation in the capital of provincial goldsmiths was summed up with the predictable bias of a London man who was, however, little less severe with his fellow city-dwellers. He was a cutler and goldsmith named William Badcock, who published his *Touchstone for Gold and Silver Wares* under his initials. He wrote:

> 'Great part of the Gold and Silver Works (especially the small works) made and sold remote from London, are notoriously known to be exceedingly Adulterated and debased, and great part of what is made by the London workers and sent into the Country to the Traders there, are as notoriously known to be as bad as any.'

The Act authorising the introduction of the Britannia standard in 1697 laid down that the lion's head erased and the figure of Britannia should be substituted for the leopard's head and the lion passant. These last had for long been employed only by the London Goldsmiths' Company, so the regulation meant in effect that only they could use the new marks. The provincial men were not permitted to stamp them, and were compelled to send their work to London for assay and marking. Not only had it to be of the requisite standard of metal but its workmanship, which had also been criticised by William Badcock, would have to match that of London silversmiths. The Londoners were understandably jealous of their privileges, so would have looked hard at any wares submitted to them by outsiders.

The provincial makers were dismayed, and Parliament was petitioned by the goldsmiths of Chester, Norwich and Exeter to permit the re-establishment of their Assay Offices. This was allowed in an Act passed in 1700, which added York and Bristol to the three named above. Articles of the correct standard of metal and of satisfactory workmanship should be stamped henceforth with the lion's head erased, the figure of Britannia, the arms of the city, and a variable annual letter together with the maker's own mark.

Town marks of Chester and Exeter

The choice of date letter was left to the individual office; while London had a Lombardic ff in a shield for 1701, most of the others chose in that year a letter A of one kind or another within a triangle or some different shape. An exception was York, where successive letters had been in use since Elizabethan times and B fell due for that year. Norwich did not take advantage of the Act, as no silver was assayed there after 1697.

The manufacture of silverware in the provinces came into prominence in the mid-1760s when the Birmingham industrialist Matthew Boulton added it to his output. He had purchased land just outside Birmingham in 1761, land that was largely barren but had on it a rolling-mill powered by a stream flowing nearby. There, Boulton built his Soho Manufactory, demolishing and re-building the mill and erecting workshops, warehouses, and homes for himself and his employees. Among the successes achieved were the making of cut-steel jewellery, including setting it with plaques of painted enamel and with Wedgwood's jasperware cameos; the manufacture of ormolu, gilt bronze, rivalling the French in design and finish; and the production of silver-plated copper goods, 'Sheffield Plate', in competition with the town of its birth.

The stream driving the mill at Soho was an inadequate and often unreliable source of power in spite of being boosted by the installation of a steam engine. This was of Thomas Savery's pattern, designed as long ago as 1702, and usable only as a pump in order to raise water from below the mill to reinforce the stream. It remained for James Watt to inform Boulton of his own greatly-improved pumping engine that required much less fuel than Savery's. In a further patent of 1781 Watt described a method of producing a rotatory motion so that machinery could be driven direct, allowing Boulton and others to have all the power they could want.

In partnership, Boulton and Watt manufactured the latter's engines for buyers all over the country, but this did not hinder Boulton from further undertakings. Among them was the production of silverware, which had also started eighty miles away at Sheffield. Both towns were able to benefit from the traditional skills of their metal-workers; skills gained in Birmingham from the production of all kinds of brass goods, and in Sheffield from the making of steel and its conversion into cutlery and other goods.

The makers of silverware in both towns suffered from the delays, dangers, difficulties and expense of getting their goods assayed and marked. Everything had to be packed and conveyed to Chester, York or London; in each instance a long journey with the risk of robbery en route. In 1771 Boulton received an order for candlesticks from the Earl of Shelburne, later first Marquis of Lansdowne, who had held ministerial posts and a few years earlier had purchased the half-completed London home of Lord Bute and named it Shelburne (later, Lansdowne) House, in Berkeley Square. On 7 January Boulton wrote apologising for delay in sending the candlesticks, which had been away for assaying at Chester for twelve days and had been so incompetently re-packed there for the return journey that the 'chasing was entirely destroyed . . . it will take near a week's work to make the necessary repairs'. He indicated to the statesman his future hopes; hopes that he had apparently revealed to Shelburne as much as five years earlier and that this misadventure underlined:

> 'I am so exceedingly vex'd about the disappointment and loss which have attended the two pairs of candlesticks that altho' I am very desirous of becoming *a great Silversmith*, yet I am determined never to take up that branch in the Large Way I intended *unless powers can be obtained to have a Marking Hall at Birmingham.'*

Lord Shelburne was prominent as a member of Parliament and could be an important ally in persuading the Government to extend the existing number of provincial assay offices, although Boulton was well aware of the opposition to be expected from the London Company. He had gained the support of Sheffield, whose Cutlers' Company wrote to him in December that 'The Establishment of such an Office has been much wish'd for by the Artificers in Silver here, who for some time past have had such a project in contemplation . . .'. Early in February 1773 separate petitions from the two towns

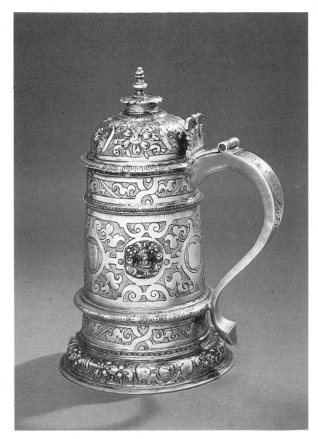

Above left
Tankard, maker's mark I R with a
quatrefoil beneath within a shield, 1602.
Silver-gilt, height 20.3 cm. *Phillips*

Above right
Tankard, 'The Lambourn Tankard',
maker's mark H G, 1661. Silver-gilt,
height 20.3 cm. *Christie's: photo,
Bridgeman Art Library.* It acquired its
name from having been presented in
1701 to St Michael and All Angels,
Lambourn, Berkshire

Right
Ewer, maker's mark C M with pellets
above and below, 1673. Silver-gilt, height
18.1 cm. *Phillips*

Left
Pair of standing cups and covers, *c.* 1715. Silver-gilt, height 66 cm. *Christie's.* The bowls bear cast replicas of the obverse and reverse of the Great Seal of England, and doubtless were made wholly or in part from the Great Seal retained by the Lord High Chancellor, the first Earl Cowper, following his resignations; he held the office on two occasions, in 1707–10 and 1714–18

Below left
Jug by Paul Storr, 1799. Silver-gilt, height 33.7 cm. *Sotheby's.* Engraved with the arms of George III and of the seventh Earl of Elgin; remembered for bringing to England the marbles from the Parthenon that bear his name and are in the British Museum

Below right
Cup and cover by Thomas Farren, 1740. Silver-gilt, height 33 cm. *Sotheby's.* Farren held the post of subordinate Goldsmith to George II between 1723 and 1742

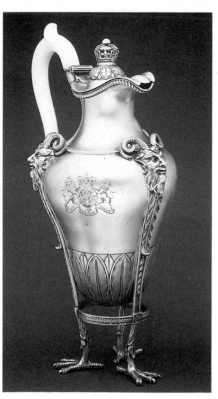

were presented to the House, and referred to a Committee for consideration.

As was expected, the Londoners objected strongly to any further possible loss of trade, but as Boulton pointed out they would suffer solely in so far as the newcomers might compete with them only 'by working better than they do and cheaper . . . [relying on] Excellence in Design and Workmanship and moderate prices'. The silversmiths were naturally jealous to protect themselves, until only recently having encountered rivalry with makers of pewter. The pewterers employed marks closely resembling those on silver, and unscrupulous traders took advantage of the fact. There were continual complaints about the marks, but rarely with any effect. However, by the early 1770s the pewter trade had declined, the metal being supplanted rapidly by improved types of pottery.

Recently, a fresh rival had appeared: Sheffield Plate, an imitation of silverware made by fusing Sterling silver to a copper base. Makers of it, like the pewterers, had a tendency to stamp their products with marks more or less like those used at the assay offices, with the result that purchasers might be forgiven for being confused as to exactly what they were buying. Externally there was little or no visible difference between an article made of Plate and one of Sterling silver, but the former was noticeably cheaper and for that reason gaining in popularity.

Petitions for and against the Birmingham and Sheffield proposals were presented and discussed, and a Bill was duly passed by both Houses. The Royal Assent being received on 28 May, no time was lost in establishing the two assay offices. Boulton stayed on in London attending to details, leaving there in the early hours of Sunday, 30th, noting in his diary: '. . . arriv'd at Soho ye Monday before 8 in ye morning', to be greeted by the ringing of the bells of Handsworth church.

'The Guardians of the Standard of Wrought Plate in Birmingham' chose as their town mark an anchor, and for the twelve months from July 1773 used a Roman A in an angular shield as their first date letter. In addition was the lion passant denoting Sterling standard and the personal stamp of the maker, while from 1784 to 1890 the monarch's head denoted that duty had been paid. The Sheffield Guardians used a crown as their town mark with an Old English E for their first date letter, and the other marks as at Birmingham. Oddly and confusingly, the Sheffield date letters were not always in alphabetical order or of a uniform face; thus, the 1791 Old English P was followed in 1792 by a lower case u and in 1817 the Roman T was followed in 1817 by X, with V occurring in 1819. The letter was changed annually on the first Monday in July.

Marks in use at Birmingham (*above*) and Sheffield (*below*) in 1773–4

Scottish silversmiths are known to have been practitioners of the craft from at least the fifteenth century, regulations for marking being in effect from 1457. In 1483 an Act coincided with the presentation of a petition by the silversmiths of Edinburgh, who were at that date associated with blacksmiths and others who wielded a hammer in the prosecution of their work and were known collectively as Hammermen. Two years later it was ordained that a deacon (president) and a searcher should be appointed, and that all wares should

Edinburgh town mark

Edinburgh thistle in use from 1759

Glasgow town mark

Glasgow Sterling mark

bear the mark of its maker as well as those of the deacon and the town. In 1586 the Edinburgh men were granted their status, which acknowledged their separate standing from the Hammermen. The town mark was taken, as was usually the case, from the arms of the burgh: a triple-towered castle.

Canongate, up the hill from Holyrood Palace and now a part of Edinburgh, was once a separate burgh with its own guilds. That of the silversmiths employed a mark in the form of a stag's head, but examples of its use are scarce and output seems to have ceased altogether by *c.* 1835.

As the proportion of the Scottish population able to afford silver was not large, so the number of suppliers was small. In the late seventeenth century it was noted that their distribution in the country was as follows: Edinburgh, *c.* 25; Glasgow, five; Aberdeen, three; Perth, Inverness, Ayr, Banff and Montrose, one apiece.

The silversmiths of Glasgow, who were also associated with Hammermen, were incorporated in 1536. A list of members over the years 1616 to 1717 has survived, but earlier and later ones have disappeared. Likewise plate of early date no longer exists, all or most of it having been given patriotically to finance military ventures, offensive or defensive.

The use of date letters began at Edinburgh in 1681, earlier wares being datable only by the deacon's mark from knowledge of his tenure of office. In the same year the mark of the official assayer was substituted for that of the deacon, and in 1759 the assay master's initials were in turn supplanted by a thistle. The monarch's head denoting the payment of duty was employed between 1784 and 1890, as was the case in England.

The date letter appeared in Glasgow also in 1681, but ceased to be used *c.* 1710, not being resumed on a regular basis until 1819 when an assay office was established. From 1819 a lion rampant was adopted officially to denote Sterling standard. In the interval there was a sporadic use of various letters, which was not out of the way in Scotland. There, the system of marking so often seems to have been haphazard, although there were probably very good reasons at the time for what now appears eccentric.

Sir Charles Jackson listed a number of towns, in addition to Edinburgh and Glasgow, where goldsmiths were established and marked their work, but some of them have been found to be inaccurate and unconnected with Scotland. The full list of those he gave was: Aberdeen, Arbroath, Ayr, Banff, Dundee, Elgin, Greenock, Inverness, Montrose, Perth, St Andrews, Stirling, Tain, and Wick. Later researchers have listed further locations but these, like the foregoing, do not include date letters among their marks. The date of manufacture has to be assessed from the style of the article or a knowledge of the working-span of the maker, but this last is possible only in those instances where he has been identified.

In Ireland a number of goldsmiths were named in a twelfth-century document and in 1498 there was a reference to a guild, which was granted a charter at a later date. The existence of the charter is known from an application made by the guild in April 1557 for a copy of the original that 'by chance was burnt'. The City

Council at Dublin ordered in 1605 that each maker should have an individual mark, that all plate offered for sale after 1 January 1606 should be assayed and if of Sterling standard bear marks depicting 'a lion, a harp and a castle' in addition to that of the maker. This lasted until 1637, when the first-noted group was replaced by a crowned Irish harp and a date letter.

From 25 March 1730 a duty of sixpence per oz was levied on new silverware and to denote payment a further mark was legalised. It took the form of a figure of Hibernia: a seated lady liable to be confused at a glance with Britannia, except that Hibernia has beside her a harp instead of a shield and holds in her right hand a short staff in place of a trident.

Dublin Hibernia and harp marks

In practice, many items of silver that paid duty and bear the Hibernia mark do not have a date letter, although an exception occurred in the case of table spoons and table forks which are almost invariably stamped correctly. No explanation for this has been found, and it means that much eighteenth-century Dublin silver can only be dated approximately. It has been noticed that there were from time to time slight variations in the design of both the harp and Hibernia; as each punch became worn or sustained accidental damage it was replaced by a fresh punch that differed in minor details from its predecessor. An attempt has been made to chart the years in which certain identifiable punches were in use by noting their appearance on inscribed or otherwise datable pieces. For example, a stringless harp has been dated as *c.* 1745, and the Hibernia of 1767–9 holds what looks like a tree-branch with four prominent twigs growing on it.

In 1807 the sovereign's head replaced Hibernia as the duty mark but both continued to be used, Hibernia becoming accepted as the Dublin town mark. After 1890, as in England, the duty ceased to be levied and the Queen's head was henceforth omitted. Jackson lists the marks of goldsmiths in Dublin, Belfast, Cork, Galway, Kinsale, Limerick and elsewhere, and for full measure appends a 'Table of Unascribed Irish Provincial Marks'. Additionally, underlining the complexity of the subject and the questions remaining unanswered when he wrote, he concluded his 700-page volume with a page of marks that could not be allocated definitely to any of the three countries: England, Scotland or Ireland.

One further mark deserves a mention although it does not appear on English-made silverware, but it is by no means an uncommon one. An Act of 1883 made it compulsory for imported foreign-made plate to be assayed and marked in the current manner, but with the addition of a capital F in an oval escutcheon. This endured until 1904, when the regulations were altered and a new series of Assay Office punches was introduced.

The dates when the English and other provincial assay offices were established is not always known for certain, and there is no doubt that silversmiths were at work at the various places long before receiving official recognition in the form of regulation. Apart from the offices that came and went in the smaller towns, a number of those in major cities have closed in modern times owing to a lack of continued demand for their services. This took place at Chester in

1962, Exeter in 1883, Glasgow in 1964, Newcastle in 1884, and York in 1858. Norwich ceased operations soon after 1700 and Bristol would seem to have been closed not long afterwards.

In 1697 and again in 1738 it was enacted that certain articles need not be assayed or marked, although it is found sometimes that they were dealt with in the normal manner. The principal criteria were weight and size: 'things which by reason of their smallness or thinness, are not capable of receiving the Marks, and not weighing 10 dwt. of Gold or Silver each'. In addition, a number of articles were specified, including: buttons, thimbles, coral sockets and bells (for babies' rattles and teethers), book-clasps, 'nutmeg-graters, very small', pencil and needle cases, and mounts on bottles. The list was amended in 1790 and some fresh items added, including any weighing under 5 dwt each *except* mounts for glass bottles, buttons, bottle tickets (better known nowadays as wine labels), small spoons and ladles, buckles and mounts for cabinets, knife cases, tea caddies, bridles, etc. This meant that the foregoing had to be assayed and hall-marked and duty became payable. A further amendment of 1798 meant that watch cases were exempted and made free of duty. As time went on, further regulations were made, altered or abolished, and the rate of duty was gradually raised until finally it was abolished altogether from 1 May 1890. Thenceforward the sovereign's head no longer appeared, although it has been revived during recent decades for commemorative articles. Apart from these exceptions it can be borne in mind that any piece of silver stamped with a Royal likeness can only have been made between 1784 and 1890.

Sterling silver was worth about 6s (30p) an oz in the eighteenth century, and it might be thought that a duty of 6d (2½p) an oz, or about 8 per cent, was a trifling matter. Some of the silversmiths, and doubtless also their customers, thought otherwise, and there were attempts to dodge the levy by making an article superficially comply with the law. This was done by cutting out the correctly marked area of an unwanted or unfashionable item and incorporating the fragment in their own work. Alternatively, a small object would be submitted for marking and then have the marked portion attached to a larger and more costly piece. In the first instance the duplicity is usually revealed by a discrepancy between the style of the piece and the date of its marks, but the same does not apply in the other case.

Even the eminent Paul de Lamerie was not above practicing such a deceit and a fine ewer in the Victoria and Albert Museum was found to bear its marks on a disc soldered in place between the foot and the base of the body, whereas they should have stamped directly on to the latter. These so-called 'duty-dodgers' are not commonplace, but they are an example of the type of abuse against which the Government tightened up the law and endeavoured to close loopholes as they were brought to light.

Despite the straightforward testing and marking regulations and the threat of fines and worse, other deceptions were sometimes tried. They were not limited to the transposition of marks; unscrupulous craftsmen devised all kinds of frauds that were difficult to detect. The most simple of them included the use of overmuch solder in assembling an article, or making the object from more than one grade of metal: in that case employing Sterling for the marking area and relying on the assayer not testing further afield.

Makers were not only warned about the risk of using too much solder, but were supposed to have every part of an article assayed and marked. Thus, a teapot would have to be stamped on the body and on the lid, and on the handle as well if that was made separately and pinned in place. This was not always done, and it is not too hard to find examples without their full complement of marks. Also, large and small pieces of silver bearing only a maker's marks are not rare. It has been suggested that they were made from a customer's own silver articles on which duty had already been paid and which the silversmith considered need not, or should not, pay the impost a second time. There was, however, no legal basis for such a practice, but it continued. Being a private transaction there would have been little or no chance of discovery by the authorities.

In 1773 there was a Parliamentary inquiry into silversmithing, and a number of frauds received a mention. Among the most blatant was that of putting pieces of base metal inside the handle of a tankard or a teapot. One witness, a silver refiner, stated that he never bought a tankard 'without first examining the handle as there had often been found pieces of brass, copper and solder within the handle . . .'. Evidence was given concerning recent prosecutions by the Goldsmiths' Company, of which a typical example that took place in 1767 concerned one William Chatterton. He was indicted for 'soldering bits of standard silver to tea-tongs and shoe-buckles, which were worse than standard, and sending the same to the said Company's Assay Office, in order fraudently to obtain their marks to the same'.

The Company was empowered to smash and return to its maker any sub-standard article that had been submitted and found to be below the specified standard of purity. In 1766, for example, 2227 lb 2 oz 2 dwt suffered that drastic treatment. While this appears to be a large quantity, it must be measured against the total amount assayed and passed in that year: 94 232 lb 11 oz 3 dwt.

The 'reading' of marks on old silver is normally less difficult than the foregoing may have suggested. With the aid of one or more of the books specialising in the subject the interested reader should soon acquire enough experience to tackle them with success. Sir Charles Jackson's big volume covers the most ground, listing the marks of makers throughout the British Isles as well as date letters, but it has not been revised since 1921 in spite of having been reprinted more than once. J. P. Fallon's almost-pocketable volume deals with London goldsmiths c. 1697–1837, and includes date letters. Other truly pocket-sized books confine their attention solely to date letters; the most compact of them being the one compiled by the late Frederick Bradbury. Much fresh information about London makers has been published by Arthur Grimwade, and no doubt there will be more as the years pass.

Techniques and Styles

When silver left the hands of a refiner it was in the form of a solid lump: an ingot. The ingot could be melted and poured into shaped moulds to cast it into objects, but more often it was beaten into the form of a flat sheet of a required thickness. The noteworthy ductility of silver permits this to be done, but after a certain amount of battering the crystals composing the metal become distorted, making the sheet brittle and unfit for further working. It is necessary to anneal it before continuing the process. Annealing involves the application of heat until the sheet assumes a dull red colour, which occurs at about 1000° Fahrenheit (*c.* 540° Centigrade), and then plunging it into cold water. This re-adjusts the crystals, ductility is restored and hammering can be resumed, followed by further annealing as and when required.

Conversion of ingots into sheets could be performed by hand-beating with hammers, or with a version of the old-fashioned laundry mangle with iron instead of wooden rollers. Power was employed for the purpose from the seventeenth century: a rolling mill, or 'flatting mill', being connected to a water-wheel, or driven by horses walking in a circle while harnessed to a large horizontal wheel geared to the mill. The metal was passed and re-passed through the rollers and annealed at intervals until the correct thickness was attained. Then, at the end of the eighteenth century James Watt perfected his steam engine; with its energy at his command the flatter could lay aside his hammer and anvil or release his horses, and the silversmith was able to rely on ample supplies of material of consistent quality.

The silver flatters were a distinct trade, and according to John Culme made their appearance in London in the 1760s. He states that Benjamin Godley, a gold and silver flatter, had premises in Newgate Street in 1767, and the firm of Christopher Scott and Robert Kirton were in Giltspur Street, Smithfield, in 1775. In that year they were engaged in building two houses in the adjoining Ball Court, which they duly occupied. Robson's classified London *Directory* of 1821 has five entries under the heading of 'Flatting Mills' without specifying the metals they rolled, and among them are Kidder and Nevill of Ball Court who presumably were continuing the business established there by Scott and Kirton.

Hammering was used also in forming cups, bowls and similar vessels, the sheet metal being carefully shaped against a suitable support. This could be a bag of sand or a hollowed block of wood that allowed curvature to take place while preventing splitting. Further shaping was achieved against a series of iron stakes, hammering carefully to ensure the article acquired an even thickness over the entire surface. The marks made by the hammer were removed by planishing, using a flat-faced planishing hammer.

A teapot body would take a full working-day to complete, but cylindrical and conical wares, for example some coffee pots, were less time-consuming. They were formed by shaping a cylinder or cone from a sheet, then soldering the seam and insetting a round base.

Casting was the other important technique, achieved either by pouring the molten metal into a shaped mould formed in special sand or by what is termed the lost wax (or *cire perdue*) method. The principle of the latter involves making a model in wax that is then encased in clay. When it has hardened it is heated and the wax poured out through a hole left for the purpose, and which is used for the introduction of molten silver to replace the wax. Finally the clay is broken away and the casting filed and polished to remove any imperfections.

Both planishing and casting could have been carried on in the silversmith's own workshop, especially if he was in a large way of business, but it was possible to contract-out either of them to specialists. In the 1790 *Universal British Directory* are the names of a half-dozen such craftsmen; there may well have been many more who were ignored as being beneath the notice of the compilers. Those who gained an entry were:

Thomas Laver, Silver Planisher, 24 Noble Street, Foster Lane

Joseph Richardson, Silver Polisher, 2 St Martin'-le-Grand

Mary Stroud, Silver Polisher, 37 Gutter Lane

Two-handled cup and cover, maker's mark I A in a dotted circle, 1667. Height 16.5 cm. *Phillips*. An example of the use of a pierced and chased sleeve decorating a vessel

Michael Barnett, Brassfounder and Silver Caster, 36 Cock Lane

William Briggs, Silver Caster, 4 Racquet Court, Fleet Street

William Halliday, Caster in Gold and Silver, Cox Court, Little Britain

All were situated in the City and most were not far distant from Goldsmiths' Hall, Foster Lane, just north of Cheapside, the focal point of silversmithing.

The foregoing is no more than the briefest outline of the processes employed in making silver articles. It was usually necessary to add decoration in addition to any that had been cast, the most widely employed being chasing or embossing. Strictly speaking, the term chasing applies to work done on the outer surface of an article to give sharpness to the primary embossing or *repoussé* work executed from the back. It is carried out with the use of a hammer and punches, the latter variously shaped and principally with blunt or rounded ends. As with all hammering the work has to be supported, and annealing is necessary at intervals. In the nineteenth century steam power encouraged the use of stamping with steel dies, which permitted the rapid reproduction of sharply-defined patterns in quantity.

A special use of chasing that originated in Germany had a brief vogue in England, and involved making a plain vessel and fitting it with a pierced and chased sleeve; in many instances the silver casing contrasting with the gilt background visible through the openwork spaces. The making of such pieces was a highly skilled operation and likely to have been costly, which may be the reason why the fashion lasted only for a short period around 1670. Equally possibly, the work can all have been done by one man who may have been an immigrant specialising in the technique he had learned abroad.

Piercing, which has just been mentioned, has both decorative and practical functions and was carried out with a fine saw. It graced the sides of bread or cake baskets, the lids of casters and the bowls of strainers. In conjunction with chasing, piercing was often used for Irish dish rings.

Chasing pushed the metal into the desired pattern but did not remove any during the process. It could be described as modelling, while engraving, which was often used in company with chasing, had much in common with the making of copper-plates for printing in relying on the physical removal of some of the silver. Engraving was performed with the use of a steel burin or graver with a sharp working-end and a rounded wooden handle. This fitted the palm of the operator's hand as he pushed it along the surface, digging out a thread of metal as he proceeded.

Due to the researches of Charles Oman, his publication of articles and a book on the subject, there is a fair amount of information concerning English engravers and their work. The most famous of them is the artist William Hogarth, who not only painted in oils but made engravings, and although his name has for long been linked with some pieces of engraved silver there is no positive proof that he did the work. However, there is no doubt about the fact that he was apprenticed to a silversmith named Ellis Gamble, of Blue Cross Street, Leicester Fields. Despite the lack of certainty, there is much

Trade card of Ellis Gamble engraved by William Hogarth (1697–1764). The artist was apprenticed to Gamble in 1713

argument in favour of Hogarth as the engraver of the Walpole salver in the Victoria and Albert Museum.

In his book, *English Engraved Silver*, Charles Oman gives the names of many men who were apprenticed in order to learn the art of engraving, and became Freemen of the Goldsmiths' Company. Little is known about their work as it was signed only exceptionally but there is always a possibility of fresh discoveries. Two names can be added from the pages of the 1790 *Directory* quoted from earlier:

Thomas Caney, Engraver and Chaser, 82 Wood Street

Francis Legrix, French plate-worker, Gilder and Silver-plate Engraver, 33 Long Acre

The last-named, who capitalised on the cross-Channel origin of his name, offered a wider than usual variety of services. Among them was that of gilding: the application of a coating of gold to all or part of a piece of silver. It was executed with a mixture of powdered gold and mercury, brushing the amalgam on the article where it was required. The article was then heated to drive off the mercury in the form of a highly poisonous vapour. The gold remained and could be left matt or burnished brightly. Gilders must have been relieved in the 1840s when electro-plating was perfected and the risk to health from inhaling noxious fumes was no longer present.

Occasionally use was made of 'cut card work': a technique that had the dual role of being ornamental as well as serving as a reinforcement. It took the form of shaped pieces of sheet silver, resembling the cut card of its name, soldered where greater strength was required. This could be round the base of a cup or where the handle and spout were joined to the body of a tea or coffee pot. Although introduced somewhat earlier, it was especially popular during the period when the use of Britannia standard metal was compulsory, the silver being softer than Sterling and requiring vessels to be given thicker walls unless potentially weak spots were reinforced in some way.

Dutch and German silversmiths were highly adept at chasing. In the first half of the seventeenth century in Holland, members of the Van Vianen family had been widely famed for their proficiency in the art, no less than for the individual style in which much of their work was executed. One of the family, Christian van Vianen, is known to have visited England for a short while in 1630 and for a more lengthy stay in 1633, after which he returned to his native land by 1647.

It is not known why Christian should have come to England, but he may have been inspired to seek Royal patronage by the example of his uncle Paul at the Court of Rudolf II at Prague. Or he could have been summoned by Charles I, as the King ordered payment to him in 1630 of an annuity of £30, raised in 1636 to £40, and in 1633 allowed him the sum of £100 towards the expense of bringing himself and his family from Utrecht.

Among Van Vianen's commissions was one for a handsome and costly silver-gilt set of altar plate for the Knights of the Order of the Garter at St George's Chapel, Windsor. The set was ordered in 1634 and delivered in full by 1639 at a total cost of £1546 6s; in the words of Charles Oman 'the whole weighed 2807 oz. 12 dwt. and must have been superb'. Unfortunately, the entire set fell victim to the Civil War; it is known that on 24 October 1642 it was looted by a Captain Fogg, thenceforward vanishing from sight and record.

Perhaps because of his Royal patronage or because his work was specially commissioned and not sold over the counter, Van Vianen did not submit it for marking at the Assay Office. No hall-marked examples of his making have been recorded; instead, some are engraved with his name and often also with the date. An important inkstand that is typical of his style can only be attributed as it is unsigned, it bears the stamped initials A I. They probably stand for Alexander Jackson, who may have been concerned in supplying it.

The style with which the Van Vianen family is closely linked has been named Auricular because it is dominated by shapes resembling the human ear, but it also incorporates grotesque human, animal and fish forms that fascinate some people while disgusting and dismaying others. The various components merge into a rippling *mélange*, and their appearance has been described as 'gristly'. It has been suggested also that its exaggerated elements owed their

inspiration to the dissecting-room, so that it has also been dubbed the Visceral style.

The style originated in Italy, but in silverware it was developed and exploited by Adam van Vianen (*c.* 1565–1627), father of Christian, who published a volume of Adam's designs in 1650. The Auricular was confined principally to the Van Vianens, but was used also by another Dutch silversmith, Jan Lutma, of Amsterdam. An immortality was conferred on him by Rembrandt's portrait etching, which shows Lutma seated in a tall-back chair, with a silver dish in the very style beside him on a table.

The limited popularity of the style in England was doubtless due to attention being directed at the time to more pressing affairs. At the Restoration new patterns made their appearance, having originated across the Channel and reaching England from Holland. They featured flowers and leaves, the latter being the spiky acanthus and the former the tulip that had earlier caused such an extraordinary furore in Holland. Acanthus leaves appeared on their own, for example, in a vertical row round the base of a vessel, or in conjunction with cupids, birds, flowers, fruit and leaves interspersed among scrolling plant stems. The last is a variety of ornament named arabesque on account of its eastern origin, which reached Europe through Venice when that seaport was the centre for trade throughout the Mediterranean.

Another, less complex, chased pattern took the form of fluting or reeding and, very often, elaborate cartouches framing spaces for engraved arms and inscriptions. Along with the foregoing were various mouldings, of which the most common was gadrooning: a

Above left
Design for a silver jug by Adam van Vianen (*c.* 1565–1627). It was published by his son, Christian, in 1650

Above right
Portrait of Jan Lutma by Rembrandt Harmensz. van Rijn (1606–69). Etching, 19.5 × 14.5 cm. The print was executed in 1656

pattern of radiating short ribs known sometimes as knurling or nulling. The background to chased ornament was often stamped with a fish-scale design or with closely-placed dots that produced a matt effect.

Engraving, other than of an owner's arms, was less in evidence, exceptions occurring in the case of flat surfaces, such as the bodies of cylindrical tankards that were decorated with chinoiseries. These patterns were English adaptations of the paintings on imported Chinese porcelain, depicting mock-Orientals with a charm for English eyes which was no less than that of the originals. The vogue for the Far East had been increasing in the seventeenth century and reached a peak during the final decades with vast importations of blue-decorated ware, popularly known in due course as Nankin. The majority of supplies reached the West through Rotterdam, being distributed from there throughout the mainland and to the British Isles. The fascination of the Orient never completely vanished and in the case of later silver took such forms as a scene of tea-making on the side of a caddy or the figure of a Chinaman as the finial of a teapot.

With the accession to the throne in 1688 of William III came signs of a change in style affecting the applied arts. Although he was born and bred in Holland and Dutch fashions might have been expected to cross the Channel with him, this was not the case. The earlier Dutch 'invasion' with Charles II had run its course, and the whole of Europe was now under the influence of the Sun King, Louis XIV of France.

Having decided in 1685 that everyone in his country was there and then of the Catholic faith and freedom of worship no longer a necessity, Louis revoked the Edict of Nantes that had protected the latter. This Act gave release to the long-simmering repression of the Protestants, who were gradually and with growing vigour driven out of France. In the space of a few years no less than 400 000 men, women and children are said to have left the country for lands where their beliefs did not invite persecution, torture and death. Many of these people, known in France since the sixteenth century as Huguenots, were skilled at various trades, including silversmithing, and many of them settled in the Netherlands. Thence, a number came to London, where they were able to establish themselves if only because of the high standard of their workmanship. Additionally, they had a knowledge of current fashions; the catch-phrase 'the latest from Paris' intriguing clients at that period just as in later days, and in spite of the fact that the majority of the refugees came from provincial towns.

Predictably, the London silversmiths did not welcome the intruders, who found it difficult to set themselves up in business. In order to market their work it had to be assayed and marked in the usual manner or risk seizure, and the Goldsmiths' charter permitted the Company to deal only with work submitted by their Freemen. A long battle ensued, starting in July 1682 when the Lord Mayor presented to the Company an order requiring it to admit Pierre Harache to the Freedom. This could not be refused, and after paying the necessary fees Harache became the first of a long line of distinguished Huguenots active in London. There was a similar request concerning Jean Louis, but his admission was delayed for several months before being granted. Things then remained quiescent until December 1687, when three more Huguenots took out denisation (naturalisation) papers and duly became Freemen.

Others among the new arrivals adopted various devices to circumvent the City rule that only Freemen of one of the Companies might trade within its boundaries. One of them was to have a workshop in one of the places known as liberty areas: for example, at Blackfriars, the site of a one-time monastery where the strict regulation did not apply. The state of affairs was changed in 1697, when it was declared that Blackfriars lay within the jurisdiction of the City and did not enjoy special privileges. Alternatively, a Huguenot might persuade one of the Freemen to submit the alien's work with his own and have both stamped at the same time. No doubt this was done in return for payment although it was against the rules of the Company.

The principal feature of the newly-introduced French style was its supplanting of chased ornament by casting. In place of the

Tankard, maker's mark W A in monogram, 1683. Height 10.1 cm. *Bonhams.* An example of chinoiserie engraving

Tankard, maker's mark G C, *c.* 1690.
Height 15.9 cm. *Christie's.* Cut-card
ornament is applied on the lid and where
the handle joins the body

ubiquitous acanthus was a series of upright straps, shaped and with raised patterns of masks and shells, that performed the decorative and practical functions of cut card work, but in a more ornamental manner. Equally, the Huguenots could adapt their skills to satisfy those clients preferring pieces of severely simple design with rounded or faceted surfaces in the so-called 'Queen Anne' manner.

It is to be noticed that the earlier cup raised on a tall foot went out of favour, to be replaced by a large-bowled vessel on a short base and with two handles. It sometimes had a matching separate dish and was usually fitted with a domed cover. By *c.* 1700, this type of cup, sometimes called a porringer, began to be supplanted by a more imposing two-handled cup and cover on a slightly taller base and of a greater weight of metal than its predecessors. This last form was greatly favoured by the Huguenot makers, who frequently embellished the lower part of the bowl with distinctive applied vertical bands.

The spread of fashions throughout Europe was fostered by the publication of books of designs that circulated widely. A number of them had been issued in France in the 1670s, some of which were soon reprinted in English versions, circulating in London and farther afield. J. F. Hayward pointed out that they would have remained in use for many years, and their inspiration is to be detected in articles made two or more decades after the designs were first published.

Cup and cover by Pierre Platel, 1707.
Height 24.8 cm. *Christie's.* Applied cast
strapwork has been used on the lid and
round the base of the bowl

This is especially the case with engraved decoration, which was the subject of the majority of the printed designs. With the arrival in London of the Frenchmen, engraving began to return to prominence after having been little seen since the days of Elizabeth. This may have come about for several reasons: because the immigrants were adept at the work; because the public welcomed a change from chased ornament; or because the Britannia standard metal, compulsory since 1697, was less amenable to chasing and ideal for engraved work.

The best-known of the French engravers is Simon Gribelin, who came from Blois, to the south-west of Paris, where the magnificent château was once a royal seat. Resident in England from the 1680s, he published in due course his first book of designs for patterns for the cases of watches, from which he progressed to decorating snuff boxes and then salvers and dishes. All Gribelin's work is of a distinctively high quality, and a number of pieces are signed. He worked for several makers, but it is not always possible to attribute unsigned pieces as they may have been executed by others who used his published designs.

It is possible to view a petition that was submitted to the Goldsmiths' Company in 1711 as a tribute to the Huguenots. Signed by no less than 53 members it drew attention to the low state of the craft, and laid this at the door of the immigrants. These men, it stated, worked such long hours and for such low rates that they had undermined the long-established Londoners, one of whom was being prosecuted for loading his work with overmuch solder in order to wrest a living. In due course, all worked amicably together, but the arrival and eventual settlement of the foreigners gave vitality to English silversmithing and did much to ensure its enduring fame.

The introduction and spread of the habits of drinking tea, coffee and chocolate during the last quarter of the seventeenth century proved to be of lasting benefit to silversmiths. When the beverages were introduced nothing was available from which to serve and imbibe them, and all required the creation of new forms of vessels. Tea was soon accompanied to the West by porcelain pots that served as models for versions in silver, while coffee and chocolate were duly poured from pots influenced by the shapes of Turkish ewers. The taking of tea eventually led to the addition of cream jugs, sugar basins and tongs, caddies and, for a short period until it was realised that fingers need not suffer scorching, cups and saucers.

In the early decades of the eighteenth century a fresh style began to sweep through Europe in the manner of an epidemic: the *rocaille* or rococo. Its elements came from the features of that rustic cave, the grotto, the abode of a real or mythical hermit. Seashells conjured up the mystery of the ocean, lichens enhanced the air of fantasy, and dripping water or icicles added to the general mixture of the unexpected, all of them linked by S and C scrolls. The final effect was of asymmetry but with an indefinable cohesion, and paramount was an illusion of restlessness and movement. It was in complete contrast to the solid and orderly baroque that preceded it.

As with other styles that came and went, it is well-nigh impossible to locate a beginning in time or place. Certainly, so far as rococo

A Book of Ornaments usefull to all Artists
by Simon Gribelin, 1700. This the
title-page of the book

Tureen, cover and stand by Juste-Aurèle
Meissonnier, Paris, 1734–6. Length of
stand 45 cm. *Cleveland Museum of Art:
photograph, Christie's.* One of a pair
made for the Duke of Kingston

Surtout and two Tureens for the Duke of
Kingston, one of the engravings in
Meissonnier's *Oeuvre* published at Paris
in *c.* 1742–51. The actual tureen
illustrated is seen on the left

silver was concerned the style was fully developed in Paris by the early 1740s, and the man responsible for its exploitation was Juste-Aurèle Meissonnier. He was born of French parents in Turin in 1695, reaching Paris by 1720 where six years later he was elected a Master by the guild of goldsmiths. His identified work is extremely rare; all that is recorded are a candelabrum, a snuff box and a pair of tureens.

The tureens, made between 1734 and 1736, are in the full rococo manner, each modelled with swirling curves and scrolls and with life-like foliage, vegetables, fish, crustaceans and a partridge. They were made, together with a table centrepiece which has disappeared, for an English nobleman, the Duke of Kingston. He was educated at Eton and in Paris, and when there would have ordered the articles from the man holding the position of *dessinateur de la chambre et du cabinet du roi* at the Court of Louis XV. The Kingston suite was depicted on one of the 74 sheets of engravings of Meissonnier's work, which included silverware, furniture and interior decoration, sculpture and much else, published in *c.* 1740.

Incidentally, an unusual story attaches to the two tureens. When the Duke died in 1773 his personal belongings were bequeathed to his widow, the former Elizabeth Chudleigh who was notorious for her behaviour both in public and private. She eventually bought an estate near St Petersburg, taking with her many of the Kingston

'A Candlestick' designed by William Ince and engraved by Mathias Darly for Ince and Mayhew's *Universal System of Houshold Furniture*, 1762

valuables, including the Meissonnier tureens. Although she left to her nephew by marriage these articles and a few others, they were not returned to him in England but were seized and sold in Russia to pay her debts. They virtually disappeared from sight and record until disposed of in Paris in 1893 by a Russian collector. Again they vanished, to re-appear at a Christie's auction at Geneva in 1977. They were bought jointly by the Thyssen-Bornemisza Stiftung and the Cleveland Museum of Art, each selecting one and agreeing that the Stiftung's example should be on extended loan to the Museum so the two could be seen together.

It was at about the time when Meissonnier's designs were published that the rococo began to appear in England, and was first to be seen in silverware; predictably from the hands of makers of Huguenot origin. It was not until the early 1740s that engraved designs in the style were issued in London, most of them showing decorative motifs for adaptation by craftsmen and others concerned with applied arts of all kinds. The asymmetrical scrolls and other elements were incorporated henceforth in the cartouches framing coats of arms and in the cast and applied ornament and basic shapes of vessels, candlesticks and other silver.

A parallel change was taking place in cabinet-making where the styles current during the reigns of Queen Anne and George I were superseded by the work of Thomas Chippendale. Most marked was the contrast in looking-glass frames, with the severe architectural styles of William Kent and others giving way to the rococo fantasies of Lock and Copland to reach a peak of excitement in the hands of Thomas Johnson.

William Kent designed not only buildings, his best-known remaining works being Houghton Hall, Norfolk, and The Horse Guards, Whitehall, but also the furniture to go in them and in a few instances silver. In this, he was followed by others whose principal field of activity was cabinet-making. Chippendale, the most eminent of English furniture designers and makers, included a few pieces of silver among the furniture depicted in his *Gentleman and Cabinet-maker's Director* of 1754. Johnson showed some pieces of silver that are no less fanciful than the furniture in a book of his designs entitled *One Hundred and Fifty New Designs*, first issued in 1758 and reprinted three years later. In or about the same year the London firm of Ince and Mayhew published a selection of their furniture designs, and among the chairs, tables and so forth was:

> 'A rich candlestick or Girandole, which if executed in wood gilt, in burnish'd gold, or Brass, would be extremely grand, and might be equally the same executed in Silver, proper for a Stand or Marble Table.'

Whether anyone attempted to translate into metal the designs of Chippendale, Johnson or Ince and Mayhew remains unknown, as in all three instances no example has been recorded.

Kent, who died in 1748, made use of the classical motifs and proportions employed by the sixteenth-century Italian architect, Andrea Palladio, and in the 1760s, when Johnson's brand of rococo was at its height, these began to reappear. The man responsible for the revival was another architect, the Scottish-born Robert Adam, who increased his professional knowledge by visiting Italy and studying the buildings there. This was in 1754, when he was 26, and he travelled in the area for a period of three years. In the course of his journeyings he met French and Italian artists and others who were eagerly discussing and developing a new style: the neo-classical. It embodied the results of research into the classical past, much of it following recently-conducted excavations. They revealed how the people had actually lived in their homes and the types of homes and surroundings that existed; in contrast to previous knowledge that was based on such ancient structures as remained more or less intact above ground.

Robert Adam and his brothers, who crossed the Border to form a business partnership in London, are renowned for their architectural work and because they also designed the decoration and contents of the principal rooms in some of their buildings. In the latter they achieved a distinctive unity; the woven carpet matching the plasterwork and colouring of the ceiling, the carving on the chairs echoing the wall-mouldings and the gilt metal door-fittings. Among the variety of articles Robert designed was a sedan-chair for Queen Charlotte, the case for a harpsichord for the Empress Catherine of Russia, and even the knocker for the front door of one of his London houses.

With such a wide repertoire it can be no surprise to learn that he designed some silverware, although he did this for his clients and, so far as is known, not for any particular silversmith. A few specimens are known that were undoubtedly made to his designs, but the majority of articles in his style were the work of his contemporaries who, with greater or lesser accuracy, followed in his footsteps. Included in their number were the architects Sir William Chambers and James Wyatt, both of whom executed commissions for Matthew Boulton. They imitated Adam's shapes, adding the swags of husks, lengths of ribbon, winged griffins, anthemions (honeysuckle blooms) and *paterae*; these last being oval or round discs modelled with radiating flutes or ribs. Combinations of all or some of them resulted in the 'Adam style', one that for a time enjoyed a general admiration but duly outlived its popularity. In 1785 Walpole wrote critically of his interiors as 'Mr Adam's gingerbread', and six years later came the death of the man who had created the style that bears his name.

Silver of the Adam or neo-classical period relied, as earlier, on chased and applied ornament, but in addition advantage was taken of a newly-introduced type of engraving. Known as 'bright cut', it was executed by cutting or gouging-out slices at an angle to the surface to produce a pattern of shining facets. It was a type of decoration that suited the well-proportioned outlines of the articles on which it was used, and it complied with the term 'elegant' applied by Robert Adam himself to his architecture.

Towards the close of the eighteenth century there started what was to be a long drawn-out argument concerning the merits of the arts of Greece and Rome. Hitherto the Romans had had absolute approval, but now debate was leading an agreed supremacy on the

Candlestick by John Carter, 1767. Height 34.7 cm. *Leeds City Art Galleries*. From a design by Robert or James Adam

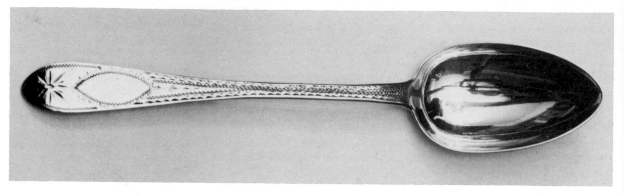

Teaspoon by Charles Marsh, Dublin, 1825. Length 15.2 cm. An example of bright-cut decoration

part of the Greeks. This came to a head with the purchase by the Government of the Elgin marbles, following a Parliamentary inquiry during which the two schools of thought aired their opinions and prejudices in public.

All of this, however, affected the design of silver, much of which was still in the neo-classical vein but in a more academic manner. Reconstructions were attempted of classical pieces, based on surviving specimens or on descriptions in the writings of ancient authors. At the same time, the Prince Regent's taste for the Far East, exemplified in the Pavilion at Brighton, gave a fillip to chinoiseries usually in the form of panels with Oriental figures in low relief. There were also interests in Egyptian and Gothic motifs, and it can be said that the decades 1800–50 saw something for everyone whatever their taste.

Some of the larger pieces of plate of the period were miniatures of marble sculptures; for example, the Warwick vase, which was reduced from its real diameter of 1.78 m into comparatively diminutive wine coolers with a width of a mere 33 cm. Some of the figures and groups forming parts of table centrepieces and candelabra would have been suitable for carving in marble on a larger scale. In fact, many of them were designed for their purpose by professional sculptors, who included the Academicians John Flaxman and E. H. Baily, and William Theed who had studied at the Royal Academy Schools. These men and others were commissioned by silversmiths who were following belatedly in the footsteps of Josiah Wedgwood. Wedgwood had sent a number of artists, including Flaxman, to Italy to seek suitable material for conversion into pottery.

An influential designer at the time was Charles Heathcote Tatham, a north-country-born architect who spent three years studying in Rome but whose career was blighted, it was said, by his propensity 'for engaging in lawsuits most unwisely with more than one of his employers'. In 1806 Tatham published *Designs for Ornamental Plate*, the first English book devoted solely to designs for silverware. In the Preface he pronounced that '... instead of *Massiveness*, the principal character of good Plate, light and insignificant forms have prevailed, to the utter exclusion of all good ornament whatever'. His words did not go unheeded and silver, like glass which was also burdened with a duty levied by weight, was employed for making cumbrous articles using quantities of material apparently without regard to cost.

At the same time as so many large and heavy pieces were being produced there was a steady output for the wider market demanding functional wares. Under pressure from the Sheffield plating industry, the industrialised workshops at Soho and elsewhere in the Midlands were busily turning out teasets by the thousand. They were well made, of thin metal and with either bright cut engraved ornament or applied patterned castings, the gauge of silver being dictated by the urgent need of competing in price with Sheffield. London and other provincial makers followed suit, although they were experiencing increasing difficulty in equalling or beating the prices of the mass-produced goods.

Ewer by Paul Storr, 1836. Height 22.5 cm. *Sotheby's, Torquay.* In the form of a Pompeian *ascos*

The death of George IV in 1830 who, despite his shortcomings in other directions, was indisputably a discerning patron of the arts, was felt as much by the silversmiths as by other makers of luxury articles. The example set by royalty and the noble and wealthy had always encouraged innovations in design and technique that were duly followed by the nation at large. Following 1830 came a decade or more of silverwares that showed few signs of innovation, relying too often on hackneyed patterns both as regards overall shapes and the designs with which they were decorated.

In many instances there were clear signs of a revival of the earlier rococo, now mis-named 'Louis XIV', with scrolls and shells vying for attention with posies of flowers. Teapots and matching teawares were spherical or oval in section, often with bulging ribbing so that each piece resembled a cantaloup melon. The Birmingham makers increasingly turned their attention to small pocketable objects, such as snuff boxes, vinaigrettes and similar pretty trifles which could be produced in quantity while not necessarily departing from a reasonable standard of quality.

The bad effects of mass-production on design began to be noticed and deplored by a discerning minority. As a result, in 1835 the Government appointed a Select Committee on Arts and Manufactures which took evidence from numerous witnesses. They included the architect J. B. Papworth, who roundly condemned the prevailing 'Louis XIV' style and further pointed out that it was in 'the debased manner of the reign of his successor'. Despite his criticism and that of others, it appeared that the general public was not displeased with the style, whether it was called after one monarch or another, and continued to patronise it.

A year after the Select Committee had been set up the Government established a School of Design, and in 1842 started the Patent Office Design Registry. The latter enabled a designer, wholesaler, retailer or manufacturer to obtain legal protection for a design over a period of three years. Apart from the formality of registration, the article had to be marked with a diamond-shaped insignia with letters and numerals indicating the name of the patentee, date and so forth. The system continued in use with minor change until 1884, when a simpler mark was introduced. The idea of such protection was to encourage new ideas, but in practice makers imitated one another as closely as they possibly could without actually breaking the law. A successful design was usually plagiarised far and wide so that it is hard to distinguish the original from the copies it inspired; only the registration mark was missing on the latter.

The next occurrence was in 1843 when the Society for the Encouragement of Arts, Manufactures and Commerce (since 1908 known as the Royal Society of Arts), which had been established in 1754 and had been moribund for many years, sprang into renewed life under the presidency of the Prince Consort. In the words of Sir Henry Trueman Wood, the Prince 'continuously impressed on the Society the necessity of its taking steps to improve the condition of the artistic industries of the country, . . . and had urged on the Society, as its proper work, the encouragement of the application of art to practical purposes'. In 1846 the first of a series of competitions was inaugurated, with prizes awarded for the best articles submitted. The most memorable of them was a china teaset made to the design of, and submitted by, an official at the Public Record Office named Henry Cole (in due time, Sir Henry) under his pseudonym 'Felix Summerly'.

Following this success, Cole founded a small firm which he named Felix Summerly Manufactures to commission the designing of items to be produced by commercial manufacturers. The goods were sold to the public in the normal way, with Summerly's taking a percentage of the profit. The goods were not confined to ceramics and among them was a silver christening mug designed by Richard Redgrave, R.A. At the same time, the Society held an exhibition of the prize-winning and other articles submitted for competition, this event proving sufficiently popular to encourage its continuance in succeeding years.

The Society then proposed a similar exhibition to be held in central London, culminating in a large-scale display on a national level to celebrate the fifth year of the shows. That was to be 1851, and from that beginning there came about the international Great Exhibition held in the Crystal Palace, Hyde Park, in that year. Cole terminated his business venture to devote his time and talents to this fresh challenge, which was fully supported by the Prince Consort.

Inkstand by John S. Hunt, 1852. Silver-gilt. *Phillips.* It is in the so-called 'Louis XIV' style, popular at the time

In the event there was a total of 13 937 individual exhibitors of whom 6556 were foreign, and their goods were seen by over 6 000 000 visitors during the 141 days when the Palace was open. From this it is reasonable to expect that the design of English silver, and much else, was duly affected by the influx of quantities of overseas products and the enormous interest shown by the general public.

The fault to be found with the Great Exhibition, and with the many similar displays that succeeded it, was that the majority of manufacturers showed goods that were representative of technical skill rather than of artistic prowess. Seldom did the two go hand in hand, and in most instances the exhibits could only be described as a tasteless and lamentable squandering of craftsmanship and materials. Nevertheless, there was no sign of objection from the mass of the people and the profits of the Exhibition made it possible for the Government to take some action at no cost to the Treasury.

From the profits the Department of Science and Art of the Board of Trade was authorised to spend £5000 on 'the purchase of such examples of manufacture, shown in the Exhibition, as it might seem desirable to acquire for purposes of study'. Further purchases with gifts and loans enlarged the collection, which was exhibited to students and others at Marlborough House, St James's, 'until more suitable premises are provided'. The Committee appointed by the Board of Trade included Henry Cole among its members, and he was also one of the two men placed in charge of the museum.

The purpose of Cole and his colleagues was to make the museum a centre for study, linked with schools of art in the capital and provinces. The idea blossomed during the remainder of the century, in the course of time resulting in a move from Marlborough House to South Kensington and the eventual erection there of a building named in honour of the Queen and the Prince, the Victoria and Albert Museum.

An effect of the newly-started museum was to draw more attention to the past as regards both design and workmanship. In the case of silver this was further encouraged by the use of electrotyping, which employed electricity to deposit the metal in making exact copies. The process had been patented by Elkington's of Birmingham in 1841, who showed at the Exhibition an 'Electrotype copy, in silver, of the celebrated cup, by Benvenuto Cellini, from the original in the British Museum'; a piece now known to have originated at Nuremberg, not in Italy.

There was a continuing output of large-sized sculptural objects for presentation on commemorative occasions or as testimonials. The opening of railways and bridges, the winning of battles, and the completion of a suitable term of years as president or chairman of a firm or an agricultural society were among the numerous events that called for a gift of solid silver statuary. No limit existed as to the range of subjects depicted: from Hindu flower sellers to Life Guards; from farm labourers tending cattle to Richard Coeur de Lion, the latter appearing on a racing-cup presented to a winning owner at Ascot in 1860.

Even in 1850 a minority was not content with the taste for such objects, and Patricia Wardle quotes from Vol. III of the *Journal of Design*:

> 'Whatever skill or excellence they may have is wrongly applied on an intractable material; the works themselves at once demonstrate this assertion. All beauty of form, all excellence of modelling, is lost in the glitter of the metal where burnishing is employed, and compositions that would have been truly works of art in bronze become almost toylike when thus wrought. If, on the contrary, the metal is not burnished, the metal is sacrificed to the art, and its value thrown away to no purpose.'

Improvement in design was still an objective. The year 1834 saw the birth of two men who later became influential as designers and propagators: William Morris and Christopher Dresser. Morris was a poet and artist who began his career in an architect's office, but eventually set up his own firm for designing interiors and selling furnishings. Some of the articles were produced by Morris and his associates themselves, all fulfilling his injunction: 'Have nothing in your house that you do not know to be useful or believe to be beautiful'.

William Morris neither made nor sold silverware, but his much-publicised ideals affected others, not least C. R. Ashbee. He was convinced, like Morris, that good could not come from industrialisation and he endeavoured to turn back the clock by a return to the medieval guild system. A workshop was established at Essex House, Mile End Road, where a small band of craftsmen produced wares that were very different from those being mass-produced by big firms. Ashbee's wares tended to be simple in form with a minimum of ornament, often having a dull surface that retained the marks of the hammer with which they had been raised from the flat sheet.

Dresser was of Scottish birth, trained as a botanist and then transferred his attention to design, working on silver from the 1860s. His pieces were plain in appearance and above all were strictly functional, his dictum being that 'Silver objects . . . should perfectly serve the end for which they have been formed'. Much of his work in the metal, which was carried out by firms in Birmingham and Sheffield, could be dated mistakenly to fifty years or more after it was produced, as his work is a surprising forecast of twentieth-century styling.

Among the events in his busy life was a visit Christopher Dresser paid to Japan, which resulted in his book *Japan: its Architecture, Art, and Art Manufactures*, published in 1882. This was at a time when there was already a vogue in the West for the country and its products, and an interest in its distinctive art was reflected in some European work; not least when they were made of silver. In England this received a fillip with the production of *The Mikado*, an instant success that ran for 672 nights following its initial performance in 1885. Japonisme did not have the wide and lasting appeal of chinoiserie, but fans, kimonos and so forth enjoyed a limited fame from about 1870 until the close of the century.

Jug by F. Elkington of Elkington & Co., Birmingham, 1885. *Sotheby's.* Designed by Christopher Dresser

Bowl and cover by C. R. Ashbee, 1899. *Victoria and Albert Museum*

The Silversmiths

In the year of the Restoration of Charles II one of the most important men in London was Robert Viner (1631–88), created a baronet six years later in 1666. He had served as apprentice and then as a partner with his uncle Sir Thomas Viner (1588–1665), who had acted as banker to the Government from the time of James I. Robert was appointed goldsmith to Charles II, a position in which he combined the roles of banker and silversmith; although the last term was used in spite of the fact that he dealt in silverware without actually being a manufacturer. This misleading application of the term continued thenceforward, causing much confusion to art historians. They have frequently found difficulty in distinguishing between producers and retailers, especially when many of the latter registered their own marks at Goldsmiths' Hall and the true maker of their goods remained anonymous.

Prior to the year 1697 the matter of identification is further complicated by a lack of records. Lists have been compiled of makers' marks recorded from actual examples, primarily by Jackson, and there are numerous references to silversmiths in old documents, but to match the mark with the maker is less simple than it may be thought. An instance is given by Charles Oman in his *Caroline Silver*:

> 'On 5th October 1655, Francis Leake, son of William Leake of Osbaston in the parish of High Ercall, Salop, was admitted a freeman of the Goldsmiths' Company, having served his apprenticeship with Henry Starkey and on 26th November 1656, his brother Ralph, who had served his apprenticeship with Thomas Viner, was made a Freeman on the same day as Robert Viner.'

Robert Viner can be assumed to have given commissions to Francis Leake, and to him can be attributed the mark F L above a bird, which is on some articles known to have been supplied by Viner.

A mark showing R L above a fleur-de-lys was once attributed to the above-mentioned Ralph Leake, probably because when the Britannia standard was introduced in 1697 a Ralph Leake registered a mark showing Le above a fleur-de-lys. However, Oman points out that there were two men of the same name, who were cousins and confusingly followed the common custom of members of a family adopting the same forename. Thus, 'it is not easy to decide whether the user of the mark R L above a fleur-de-lys was Ralph Leake I or Ralph Leake II who received his freedom in 1676 ... It is even conceivable that the cousins may have been in partnership and used the same mark'.

Among the few men whose work has been identified with reasonable certainty are Robert Smythier and John Bodendick. Smythier, whose brother William was apprenticed to Thomas Viner, was the son of Robert Smythier of Arlingham, Gloucestershire. To Robert Smythier, Junior, is attributed a good amount of surviving plate marked with S crowned. Bodendick, who signed his name on documents Bodendeick, came from Germany and was granted British naturalisation in 1661, the same year in which he married the daughter of a London goldsmith. Bodendick probably used the mark I B above a crescent between two pellets which has been found on some especially fine candlesticks and on other pieces chased in notably high relief.

Other good examples of the same technique bear the mark A M in monogram, which is identified with Arthur Manwaring. Manwaring completed his apprenticeship in 1643, and Oman records a pair of andirons with his mark and the date letter for 1696. This span of 53 years would seem to cover an unusually long working life for one man, and it is therefore possible that the mark was used successively by two owners of the same initials.

One other craftsman of the 1660s may be mentioned: Jean-Gérard Cooqus or Cockus, none of whose work has yet been identified but of whose activity there is documentary evidence. It is known that he came to England from Liège and died in London in 1697. If for no other reason Cooqus will be remembered for having supplied a silver bedstead to Nell Gwyn in 1674 at a cost of nearly £1000.

The picture suddenly clarifies with the coming into effect on 25 March 1697 of the statute raising the standard of silver. It increased the proportion of pure metal in each ounce and at the same time banned the employment of Sterling. Each goldsmith had to register a new personal mark, comprising the first two letters of his surname: for example, Le for Ralph Leake. The books in which this important information was recorded remain at Goldsmiths' Hall (with a few exceptions of later date already mentioned), so there should be only occasional room for doubt as to who made any article. In fact, a number remain defying identification, as from time to time there were practices that defeated the carefully-compiled regulations of the Company.

Reference has been made to the so-called duty-dodgers, and in addition to the products of those deliberate law-breakers were the items that bear a maker's mark overstamped with that of another man. The obliterated mark would be that of the actual producer, while the superimposed one was added either by another silversmith or by a retailer. In the case of a maker doing this, he might have received an urgent order that he filled by purchasing his requirements from a colleague with the goods already in stock; a retailer might take the same action to ensure a buyer did not know of

One of a pair of candlesticks by Jacob Bodendick, 1669. Height 31.1 cm. *Sotheby's.*

the actual maker and so was unable to go behind the retailer's back to his source. There are instances, also, of provincially-made pieces bearing overstruck London marks, no doubt because buyers placed more reliance on the latter as regards the goodness of the metal and quality of workmanship.

Further examples occurred when registered silversmiths presented the work of unregistered craftsmen for marking, pretending that it was their own. This was not uncommon with some London silversmiths who sponsored the work of the earlier Huguenot immigrants, knowing it was illegal to do so and risking the possibility of discovery. The deception is sometimes obvious by reason of the style and workmanship of a suspected object being quite unlike those normally associated with the maker.

The leading English-born silversmiths at the close of the seventeenth century were Benjamin Pyne and the brothers George and Francis Garthorne, of whose output sufficient is extant to demonstrate their skill and taste. Pyne had his workshop in St Martins Le Grand, obtaining his freedom from the Company in 1676 and rising to the office of Prime Warden in 1725. Two years later he was declared bankrupt, filling the less exalted position of Beadle on condition that he resigned all his other places. Among outstanding pieces bearing Pyne's mark is an immense wine cistern standing 96 cm in height and weighing 2056 oz, made in 1702. He also made a number of ceremonial maces ranging in date from the 1690s to one of 1722 at Winchester, as well as a wide range of other articles.

Pyne's role as Beadle included the distribution of printed notices advertising stolen property, an example of June 1731 offering a reward of two guineas for the return of a draft of £30 drawn on the Bank of England. About eighty years earlier John Evelyn took advantage of the same service in an endeavour to recover articles stolen from him by two footpads on 23 June 1652, noting in his diary:

'The next morning weary & sore at my wrists & armes [from being tied up] I went from Deptford to London, got 500 tickets printed & dispers'd, by an officer of Gould Smiths-hall, describing what I had lost, and within two daies after had tidings of all I lost, except my Sword which was a silver hilt, & some other trifles.'

The Garthornes were patronised by William III; a twelve-branch chandelier ornamented with crowned escutcheons bearing national emblems, with George Garthorne's mark and dating from c. 1700, is at Hampton Court. Francis Garthorne obtained the freedom of the Girdlers' Company by 1694 and was Master in 1718, while his brother was free of the Goldsmiths' in 1680.

From about 1690 the Huguenots gradually rose to prominence and were eventually absorbed into English silversmithing. By sheer hard work and good craftsmanship allied with an ability to get orders from important buyers they raised, or certainly maintained, the standards of the craft. The name of one of them, Paul de Lamerie, became as familiar for fine silverware as that of Thomas Chippendale for the best cabinet-making.

It has been stated that Pierre Harache was the first of the immigrants to obtain his freedom of the Company; that was in July 1682,

and five years later he became a Liveryman. His son, Pierre Harache II, gained his freedom in 1698 and following a predictable pattern the first Harache took as an apprentice one of his own countrymen, Simon Pantin. In turn, Pantin had apprenticed to him his son, also named Simon, and Augustin Courtauld, who came to England at some date prior to 1696 when he was granted naturalisation. Courtauld was one of a family of skilful silversmiths whose working lives spanned much of the eighteenth century; the name remaining alive today in the Courtauld Institute of Art in London, given to the nation in 1931 by a descendant of the silversmiths.

A good proportion of the many Huguenots who settled in London are recognised as having produced excellent work. A half-dozen may be named with brief notes of their careers, but such a list could easily be extended. The six selected are:

Peter Archambo, granted freedom of the Butchers' Company in 1720. Among his apprentices was his son of the same name. Peter Archambo I died in 1767.

Louis Cuny, obtained freedom of the Goldsmiths' in 1703, and his son, also Louis, was apprenticed to him.

Daniel Garnier, naturalised in 1687 and obtained his freedom of the Goldsmiths' twelve years later.

Basket by Paul de Lamerie, 1747. Silver-gilt, length 38.4 cm. *Colonial Williamsburg photograph.* An outstanding example of English rococo

Pierre Platel, came to England in 1688, was naturalised in 1697 and free of the Company two years later. His apprentices included Paul de Lamerie.

Philip Rollos, obtained his freedom of the Company in 1697. His son of the same name was also a silversmith.

David Willaume, came to England in 1686, being naturalised in the year following and obtaining the freedom of the Company in 1693. Among his apprentices was Louis Mettayer, another Huguenot and perhaps the brother of Willaume's wife, and his son David Willaume II. Willaume I is thought to have died at some date prior to 1728.

Many of the immigrants, including five of the six listed above, had in their personal mark the fleur-de-lys, a reminder of their country of origin.

The most esteemed of the men was Paul de Lamerie, of whom more is known than about any of his fellows. He was the subject of a detailed biography published over fifty years ago: *Paul de Lamerie: citizen and goldsmith of London* by P. A. S. Phillips, 1923. In the middle of the last century there is evidence that of all the Georgian silversmiths his reputation endured and his name, albeit mis-spelt, was not forgotten. In the catalogue of the exhibition of works of art held at South Kensington in 1860 there is a section devoted to 'Plate of English Manufacture', which runs to some 280 items. They included a pair of gilt tankards of 1732 'by the celebrated London goldsmith Paul Lamère', a silver-mounted tortoiseshell tea caddy of 1743 'the work of the celebrated Paul Lemaire', and a cup and cover of 1743 by the same.

De Lamerie was born in 1688, the son of French Protestants of good family who fled from France to the Netherlands, being brought at the age of three to London where he lived with his parents in a house at Berwick Street, Soho. In 1703 he was naturalised and almost at once apprenticed to Pierre Platel, obtaining his freedom of the Goldsmiths' in 1712 and entering his first mark. Paul de Lamerie married in 1716, was the father of six children and died at his house in Gerrard Street, Soho, in 1751.

De Lamerie is deservedly famed for the consistently high standard of his output. It is notable that he continued to use the more costly Britannia standard metal for some years after 1720, when it was no longer obligatory to do so. He did not register his mark for Sterling, showing his initials instead of the first two letters of his surname, until 1732. Among the most exuberant of his works is a pair of silver-gilt baskets at Colonial Williamsburg, Virginia. The baskets are described by John D. Davis as the most important examples of English rococo in that outstanding collection. Davis wrote:

'He [Lamerie] more than any other English silversmith, realized the rich potentialities of this decorative style. He had an unusual ability, stemming from his extreme inventiveness, to integrate form and varied ornament with rich overall decorative effect and a rhythmic play of textures.'

Pair of ewers by Matthew Boulton,
Birmingham, 1776. Height 37 cm.
Phillips. Their design has been attributed
to James Wyatt, an architect and a
member of a numerous family that
followed the same profession

In his will, the silversmith stated that unfinished articles in his workshop should be completed and sold. An auction was held, and some of the moulds for casting and other items were purchased by Phillips Garden who used them in his own work. Garden entered his first mark in 1738 after obtaining his freedom of the Company in the same year, and became a Liveryman in 1746. In 1762 his name was listed among the bankrupts in the August issue of the *London Magazine*:

Phillips Garden, of St. Paul's Churchyard, Silversmith.

He resigned as a Liveryman the next year.

Contemporary with many of the foregoing was Nicolas Sprimont, born at Liège in 1716 and who came to England some time before 1742. In that year he was married in London, entering his mark at Goldsmiths' Hall in the next year. The finest assembly of his rare and distinctive work is in the Royal collection, some of the pieces being closely related to Chelsea porcelain because of a shared use of marine forms. Indeed, Sprimont was connected with the management, and later with the ownership, of the factory from soon after its establishment in about 1743. It is thought that Sprimont worked in conjunction with the silversmith Paul Crespin, both of them having workshops in Compton Street, Soho.

The fact that Sprimont turned his attention from the one craft to the other draws attention to the fact that the retailing of silverware and porcelain was not infrequently pursued under the same roof. A confirmation of the practice is contained in an advertisement that appeared in the *Daily Advertiser* of 9 January 1750:

'BOW CHINA, to be sold by John Sutro, Goldsmith and Toyman, at the Golden Heron on the North Side, St Pauls Church Yard, at the same price as at the Manufactory, for the sake of ready money only.

Note, this China is now come to so great a perfection that it is not inferior to old Japan; and that Gentlemen and Ladies may be assur'd there is no imposition, the lowest price is fix'd on each Piece.'

By the mid-century it becomes clear that growing demand was leading to increasing signs of specialisation. For example, Robert Abercromby who registered his first mark in 1731, was a maker of salvers, the number surviving suggesting that perhaps he could have had little time to spare in which to make anything else. William Peaston, whose mark was registered with the Company in 1746, and at a later date Thomas Hannam and John Crouch concentrated their energies on the same articles. Among those who produced candlesticks were the brothers John and William Cafe, whose marks were registered in 1741 and 1757 respectively, and John Carter (1776). The latter's mark is sometimes found overstamped on that of another maker, presumably because Carter was unable to complete a commission in good time and bought from someone else in order to do so. David Hennell, the first of a long line, specialised in salts, after having served his apprenticeship from 1728 with Edward Wood, also a salt maker.

Opposite page
(above) Inkstand by Robert Hennell, 1789. Silver-gilt, length *c.* 25 cm. *Private Collection: photo, Bridgeman Art Library* *(below)* Tray by Benjamin and James Smith, 1810. Silver-gilt, length 70.8 cm. *Phillips.* Benjamin Smith was in partnership with Digby Scott 1802–9, then with his brother James 1809–16 and his son, also Benjamin, 1816–18, working mostly for the Royal Goldsmiths, Rundell, Bridge and Rundell

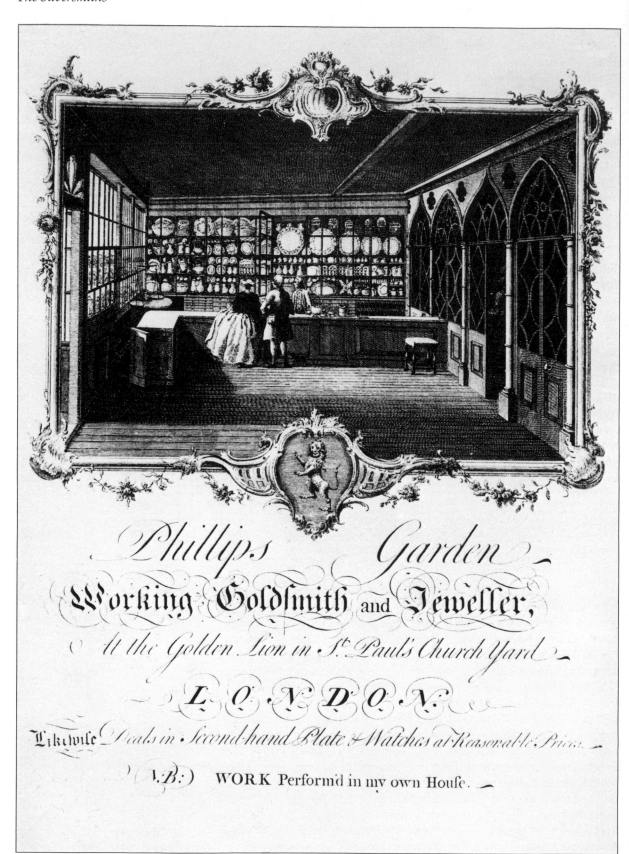

Although Joseph Brasbridge was listed in Wilkes's 1790 *Universal British Directory* as 'silversmith and cutler' at 98 Fleet Street he was, in fact, a straightforward retailer of other people's manufactures. In his autobiography he mentioned some of his suppliers, his views being somewhat coloured because most of them were understandably cautious towards him following his bankruptcy. Some of Brasbridge's reminiscences are not without interest; for instance the following, which relates to specialisation:

> The late Mr Richard Crosley, of Giltspur-street, was my principal spoon-maker; I have laid out more than fifty thousand pounds with him ... He came originally to London as a boy, and was employed by Chawner, the spoon-maker in Paternoster-row, to carry charcoal to his men; hence he was known by the name of Charcoal Dick ...

He relates a story about one of his clients who had been presented with a pair of candlesticks and wanted another pair made to match. Brasbridge passed on the order to Thomas Whipham, but the latter mistook the weight scratched under each base as referring to the pair rather than to each single article. The finished candlesticks were 'exactly similar indeed in point of pattern, but as thin as paper', so the work had to be done again. When finally completed and approved the result would have been a matching set of four candlesticks, with one pair bearing a later date mark than the other. In a similar way sets of arms, or branches, were sometimes supplied to fit earlier candlesticks and convert them when required into candelabra. Likewise, the branches would be dated differently from the bases, and would probably have been the work of two different makers.

Additions of the kind, and sets comprising items by different silversmiths at different dates are far from unknown. An example occurred in about 1740 when the Duc de Biron, a favourite of the Empress Anna of Russia, acquired a 24-piece toilet service. The various items, each decorated with a chased pattern of shells and scrolls, bear dates ranging from 1718 to 1738 and the marks of no fewer than six makers: Paul de Lamerie, Peter Archambo, Augustin Courtauld, Simon Pantin, George Johnson and Edward Vincent. In 1922 the service came into the possession of the Hermitage Museum, Leningrad, where it remains.

A further change that took place in the mid-eighteenth century concerned the man designated 'Royal Goldsmith'. From early in the sixteenth century he had been principally a banker and money-lender, any silverware supplied by him being made by others. In 1760 this changed: George III appointed Thomas Heming 'at The King's Arms in Bond Street, facing Clifford Street' to the position, and the Royal Goldsmith was a practical working silversmith with his own workshop. Heming, or Hemming as his name was spelt sometimes during his lifetime, served his apprenticeship with Peter Archambo and registered his mark in 1745. His trade card of *c.* 1765 shows several articles in the currently fashionable style, including a covered cup of distinctive pattern that is in the Victoria and Albert Museum. Heming's sons, George and Thomas, were apprenticed to

Opposite page
Trade card of Phillips Garden, *c.* 1740. It shows the interior of a silversmith's showroom; he stresses that his goods were made 'on the premises' and that he was no mere retailer

Dish by George Wickes, 1739. Silver-gilt, diameter 25.4 cm. *Christie's.* It is engraved with the coat of arms of Frederick Louis, Prince of Wales, Wickes's most important patron

him in 1763 and 1767 respectively, the former going into business with William Chawner, father of the William Chawner mentioned by Joseph Brasbridge. George Heming eventually took over the running of his father's Bond Street concern.

George Wickes, whose mark was registered in 1721 was a close rival to Heming. He set up in business in Threadneedle Street, and then in 1735 removed to Panton Street, Haymarket. By then, or not long afterwards, he was appointed 'Silversmith to His Royal Highness the Prince of Wales'; the latter being Frederick Louis, son of George II and heir to the throne, who died in 1751, pre-deceasing his father who was succeeded by the Prince's son. George II and the Prince did not see eye to eye, to put it mildly, and when the young man came to London from Hanover at the age of 21 he quickly became the focus of political intrigues aimed at the Crown. This contributed in no small degree to the family warfare.

Whatever may have been his shortcomings in other directions, the Prince had a true appreciation of the arts. His patronage was extended to the French-born painter Philippe Mercier; to the York-shire landscape-gardener, architect and artist William Kent; and to writers like Swift and Pope. On his death, the so-called 'Girl in a Swing' porcelain factory, believed to have been at Chelsea, pro-duced a touching group of Britannia mourning the loss of the Prince; the weeping figure holding a shield on which is his portrait in relief. Even if his father often kept him so short of money that he could not pay his bills, the Prince and his followers were worthwhile clients of Wickes, who duly brought considerable benefit to the Panton Street establishment.

It is fortunate that the ledgers kept by George Wickes and his successors still survive, forming the basis for the book on the firm's founder by Elaine Barr. The firm was run from 1747 in partnership with Edward Wakelin, the latter joining with John Parker and con-tinuing the business following the retirement of Wickes in 1760. Wakelin and Parker were succeeded by Wakelin's son, John, who duly took as partner Robert Garrard, and this name is retained to the present day by his successors. The 200-year run of records was found in the dusty basement when the modern firm was bought 'lock, stock and barrel' in 1952, and the Albemarle Street premises they had occupied since 1911 were being cleared for removal to Regent Street. Most of the documentary material is now in the safe keeping of the Victoria and Albert Museum.

Wickes is known to have been the maker of a gold cup to the design of William Kent, a design later engraved by John Vardy in *Some Designs of Mr Inigo Jones and Mr William Kent*, issued in 1744. The volume includes a large table centrepiece for the Prince of Wales, which survives in the Royal Collection. Hall-marked 1745, it has been altered on two occasions, in 1829 and 1847, but retains enough of its original features for its source to be recognisable.

Apart from some pieces in Kent's baroque style, most of Wickes's work was distinctly rococo, and it was not until after his retirement that signs of the neo-Classical style appeared in articles leaving Panton Street. Of the many who adopted the new style few were more successful than the Birmingham manufacturer, Matthew Boul-ton, who was rivalled closely by his neighbours at Sheffield. Many of the sketches and finished drawings used at the Soho works by Boulton and his partner, John Fothergill, are in the Birmingham Reference Library. Some of them are reproduced and discussed by Robert Rowe, who also illustrates a number of pieces made from them, as well as others from Robert Adam's own designs executed by various London silversmiths.

Among the numerous exponents of Adam's innovations, and equally a successful challenger of the Midlands makers of silver and plated goods, was Hester Bateman. Her husband, John, a maker of gold chains, died in 1760 when she was 51 and the mother of four sons and two daughters. She registered her own mark in 1761 and until 1790 when she handed over control of the business to her sons,

Design for a cup by William Kent (1684–1758). From *Some Designs of Mr. Inigo Jones and Mr. William Kent* by John Vardy, 1744

Peter and Jonathan, she ran the workshop in Bunhill Row, off Old Street in the City. It has been thought improbable that Hester Bateman was herself responsible for any of the actual silver-smithing, and that she would have employed one or more managers to supervise production.

Whoever was responsible for the output was alert to changes taking place in techniques; realising that the large-scale mechanised operations afoot in the Midlands presented a formidable challenge to the traditional expensive hand-workmanship hitherto general in the industry. The Bateman workshops kept their designs simple in outline, economised in metal by using thin sheet wherever possible, and made a speciality of decorating their wares with neat and attractive bright-cut engraving.

Judging by the amount of surviving ware bearing one or other of their marks, they found a successful formula that appealed to a wide public. The unpretentious articles allied with a woman's name still enjoy much popularity on both sides of the Atlantic. It was, incidentally, no novelty for a woman to register her own mark and ostensibly run a workshop. There are examples of the practice from early in the eighteenth century, when more than one widow of a silversmith set the pattern followed by Hester Bateman.

Silversmithing was becoming bisected: one portion of the craft catering for the rapidly increasing demands of the mass market, and the other portion ignoring expense in supplying the wealthier members of the community. The latter obeyed the call of Charles Heathcote Tatham for 'massiveness', and in no uncertain manner. The foremost firm retailing such pieces were the Royal Goldsmiths: Rundell, Bridge and Rundell, of Ludgate Hill, whose name is linked closely with that of the man named by N. M. Penzer 'the last of the goldsmiths': Paul Storr. The business was active in the 1750s as Theed and Pickett, changing to Pickett and Rundell in 1772 when the firm's shop-assistant, Philip Rundell, became a partner. He eventually purchased Pickett's share. A fresh assistant was employed from 1777, he was John Bridge who had served his apprenticeship with a jeweller at Bath and in turn became a partner with Rundell. Successive changes in partnership led in 1805 to the name becoming Rundell, Bridge and Rundell, the firm continuing to trade until 1842 when the remaining stock was disposed of in a ten-day auction. The architects of the concern's success were Philip Rundell and John Bridge, whose characters were described graphically by one of their employees.

The latter, George Fox, Junior, wrote of the two men in a manuscript now in the Library at Harvard University:

'No two men could have been more opposite in temper and disposition than were Mr. Rundell and Mr. Bridge – indeed so opposite were they that many designated them by the names of Oil and Vinegar. Mr. Rundell was naturally of a violent disposition, very sly and cunning, and suspicious in the extreme. Avarice, covetousness and meanness were so deeply rooted in him that it affected every feature of his face and entered into every action of his life! . . . In his shop he was ever the petty despotic

King, not only over his servants, but also over his partners, and all the tradespeople he employed, and swearing, scolding and noise were the order of the day, and of every day. . . . . Mr. Bridge was quite a different man. He was naturally of a timid quiet disposition . . . and he would hear any insults or brook any imposition rather than he would contend against his more violent Partner. . . . He could perform well on his own stage or amongst his Customers out of doors, for although he possessed as much Pride as any Person need have yet to any one and to every one by whom he expected to gain any thing he was apparently the most humble and obedient Person that could well be imagined, his back was exceedingly flexible and no man in London could bow lower or oftener than could Mr. Bridge.'

It was the obsequious John Bridge who gave the firm its opportunity of becoming the most important of its day, and enabled his partner to leave a fortune of £1 500 000 when he died in 1827. Bridge came from Dorset, where his cousin and namesake was a highly successful farmer. In 1789, George III who not for nothing was nicknamed 'farmer George', was convalescing at Weymouth and paid a call on Bridge, whose opinions on agriculture were well-known and respected.

In the course of a further meeting the King learned that Bridge's cousin was employed in the shop at Ludgate Hill, where the Royal interest would be greatly welcomed. In due course, the Court having returned to London, John Bridge was summoned to the Palace and in the words of Norman Penzer 'so pleased the King that he was introduced to the Queen, the whole of the Royal family, as well as many members of the Court and nobility'. Rundell, Bridge and Rundell were duly appointed 'Jewellers, Gold and Silversmiths to the Crown' and were granted similar appointments to the Prince of Wales, the Duke of York and the several Princes and Princesses of the Royal family.

John Bridge was responsible not only for the introduction of an extensive and important clientele, but probably it was he who selected William Theed as chief designer to the firm. Theed, born in 1764, was a sculptor of classical figures and groups who trained in London and Rome, returned from Italy in about 1796 and from 1799 to 1804 worked for Wedgwoods, then in the hands of Josiah Wedgwood II. He then transferred his talents from pottery to silver, was made a partner by his new employers and remained with them until his death in 1817. Two other well-known sculptors are known to have worked for Rundells: John Flaxman and Thomas Stothard, and a third, Thomas Hodges Baily, remembered best for his figure of Nelson surmounting the Column in Trafalgar Square, was chief modeller from 1816 until the business closed.

Rundell, Bridge and Rundell were retailers not manufacturers, and they began by having their stock supplied from two sources: the workshops of Benjamin Smith and Paul Storr. The former worked from 1802 to 1814 in partnership with Digby Scott, in premises at Greenwich that were apparently owned or leased by Rundells. Storr stayed the course longer, working from premises in Dean Street,

Soho, becoming a partner in the firm in 1807 and retaining his position for the ensuing twelve years. The wares originating from both sources, as well as from others known to have been used by Rundells, were invariably of the highest finish and often gilded. Ornamental details were sometimes re-used, but in different ways so that a particular decorative feature might appear on several objects. Charles Oman has drawn attention to a group that includes a piping faun and a bacchante used on some epergnes in 1812 re-appearing three years later round the stems of a pair of candelabra.

All the pieces from Storr's workshop bear his mark, date-letter and so forth in the normal manner. Some important articles were additionally engraved with the words: RUNDELL BRIDGE ET RUNDELL AURIFICES REGIS ET PRINCIPIS WALLIÆ LONDINI; translating from the Latin as 'Rundell Bridge and Rundell London Goldsmiths to the King and the Prince of Wales'. At other dates appropriate forms of the legend were used.

When Paul Storr left Dean Street the contents of the workshop remained the property of Rundells; Philip Rundell registered a mark of his own in March 1819 and John Bridge entered his in 1825. Storr took premises of his own in Harrison Street, Grays Inn Road, and in 1822 acquired a retail outlet in New Bond Street. It had been managed previously, when owned by a goldsmith and jeweller, by John Mortimer and forthwith traded as Storr and Mortimer. Storr retired in 1838 when the firm became successively Mortimer and Hunt, and Hunt and Roskell, the latter bringing it into the present century.

The privilege of being goldsmiths to the Crown meant that Rundell, Bridge and Rundell not only supplied new articles that were required, but they would be offered any surplus pieces. In this way, as related earlier, the firm acquired a considerable number of items in 1808 when the Prince of Wales wanted money to install his estranged wife at Kensington Palace. The Royal surplus was bought by, among others, the Duke of Buccleugh, Earl Brownlow, the Earl of Exeter and William Beckford.

There had always been a market for second-hand plate, although only rarely was it supplied from such an exalted source. In November 1696 John Hervey, later first Earl of Bristol, noted the purchase of some dishes and other articles for a total of £211 7s, paying £7 7s in cash and 'ye rest in old plate of my dear fathers'. In the same month he exchanged more old plate for new, and it is not improbable that all or many of these pieces would have been re-sold rather than melted by the silversmiths concerned. John Hervey bought second-hand items himself: for example on 1 April 1737, when he recorded in his diary the purchase of an epergne 'at Lord Scarsdale's sale', and in 1726 when he acquired a number of articles 'bought at Brigadier Mundens Auction of goods'. There is plenty of evidence that many other persons of all ranks followed the same practice. One silversmith, Stafford Briscoe of Cheapside, went so far as to advertise in the 1750s that he stocked old plate as well as new.

In the early 1800s old silver began to be regarded not merely as a cheap alternative to new, but its design and craftsmanship gained recognition: the collecting of old pieces for their historical and

Advertisement in *The General Evening Post*, 5 February 1751, listing second-hand silverware stocked by Stafford Briscoe of Cheapside

Tankard by John Jones, 1742. Height
21 cm. *Sotheby, King and Chasemore.*
The spout has been added and so has
the embossed and chased decoration; it
is inscribed and dated 1856, probably the
year in which the additions were made

aesthetic qualities had started in earnest. This newly-awakened interest was catered for in part by genuinely antique specimens, and partly by modern copies that more or less imitated the originals. It was far from unknown, also, for parts of old articles to be incorporated in new works with, perhaps, the stem and base of a sixteenth-century cup becoming the stem and base of an otherwise modern tazza. There appeared, too, the first signs of a custom that grew as the century progressed: that of adding chased ornament to plain articles and making them more pleasing to the contemporary buyer, but greatly lowering the value in modern eyes.

Much to the fore in encouraging the increasing liking for old silver was a dealer named Kensington Lewis, originally Kensington Louis Solomon and thought to have been of German or Dutch origin. From 1822 until about 1840 he had premises in St James's Street and was appointed Goldsmith and Jeweller to the Duke of York who became a valuable client in the years prior to his death in 1827. For new items Lewis employed a skilful silversmith, Edward Farrell who supplied, among much else, a huge nine-light candelabrum modelled with Hercules destroying the Hydra, almost 1 m in height and weighing over 1000 oz, for which the Duke paid about £1200.

At the mid-century, to be precise in 1851, there is ample evidence about what was popular and who supplied it. The well-documented Great Exhibition provides a mine of information on the subject, not only in words but with pictures of the more striking pieces on display. Class 23, shown in the South Central Gallery, comprised 'Works in Precious Metals, Jewellery, etc.' and included Sheffield Plate among the 140 separate exhibits, of which the last was the Kohinoor diamond recently acquired by Queen Victoria. The most striking and extensive of the displays were provided by the firms of Hunt and Roskell; C. F. Hancock who had been with the foregoing; and R. and S. Garrard, all of which were dominated by some of the greatly admired presentation groups made to commemorate all kinds of deeds and occasions. One of the most ambitious of them was a table-service presented to the Earl of Ellenborough, who had been appointed governor-general of India in 1841 and faced considerable difficulties with both Afghans and Chinese during his few years in the East. The catalogue description of the principal piece of the service shows that it fully reflected those eventful years:

'Asia, crowning Britannia, on a pedestal of Indian architecture, with palm-trees at the angles. Bassi-relievi of the treaty of Nankin, and views of Calcutta, Cabul and Canton. Figures of Affghan and Chinese captives, and a British sepoy. The whole supported by recumbent elephants.'

Nothing was omitted; the recipient was given a lifelike reconstruction of the happenings in his career that would have set his dinner table ablaze with conversation.

Garrards' contribution included a large ewer modelled in relief with the Labours of Hercules which was sold to the Emperor of Russia. It was described approvingly by the *Art Journal* as 'a most spirited and artistic work of its class'. In contrast to the Emperor's purchase was a dessert service modelled from water plants to be

Opposite page
Nine-light candelabrum modelled with Hercules destroying the Hydra by Edward Farrell, 1824. Height 89 cm. *Christie's.* Sold by Kensington Lewis of St James's Street to the Duke of York, son of George III

seen at Kew Gardens, shown by a firm of retailers S. H. and D. Gass of Regent Street, London. This, too, gained the admiration of the same publication, which considered 'it is quite needless to expatiate upon the taste displayed in the adaptation of these natural forms to manufacturing art'.

The big names in what was now a great industry continued to display their *tours de force* at successive international exhibitions held in this country and elsewhere. The home market expanded rapidly with the lowered price of the metal due to the finds in the United States. Public taste was satisfied by and large by copies in late eighteenth-century styles, particularly the neo-classical and weak versions in Robert Adam's manner to complement the furniture then enjoying a revival. In contrast to this was the comparatively plain work of C. R. Ashbee who attempted to defeat the inexorable advance of the machine. His scale of production was very limited, and his effort at turning back the clock had little effect at the time.

There was a continual demand during the second half of the century for all kinds of novelties, several firms concentrating on their production. The pages of newspapers and magazines, especially at Christmas, were full of references to such trifles as patent propelling pencils, vesta cases, scent bottles and so forth, neatly modelled in the forms of popular characters like Punch and Judy and human-like apes and, of course, as cats, dogs and birds or anything else likely to catch the imagination. John Culme devotes several pages to these toys; toys that would surely have been stocked by Horace Walpole's 'toy woman *à la mode*', Mrs Chenevix, had they been available in her day nearly 150 years earlier.

Above left
Cigar-lighter modelled as Punch by George Fox, 1846. Height 7.7 cm. *King and Chasemore*

Above right
Inkwell modelled as a begging retriever by Charles Rawlins and William Summers, 1850. Height 14 cm. *Bearnes, Torquay*

Opposite page
Centrepiece of the Ellenborough Testimonial. Woodcut from the catalogue of the Great Exhibiton, 1851. It was made and exhibited by Hunt and Roskell, late Storr and Mortimer, of 156 New Bond Street

A Dictionary of Silver Articles

ALTAR PLATE *See* Religious plate

APPLE CORER

The most usual form was a hollow cylindrical cover forming a handle into which the blade screwed for use; when not required the blade was reversed and screwed inside the handle. An example of late seventeenth-century make is recorded, but mostly they date from a century or more later. It is noticeable that the blades of old corers are small in diameter and of little use with a modern apple, the reason being that the old varieties of apple were comparatively diminutive.

ARGYLL or ARGYLE

A container for gravy designed to keep the liquid hot, or at least warm; no trivial matter in houses where the dining room was distant from the kitchen. It is said to have taken its name from the man for whom the first one was made: a Duke of Argyll, and as the earliest examples date from *c.* 1755, it is probable that they commemorate Archibald, third Duke, 1682–1761, who had a distinguished military and political career. There was more than one variety of argyll, employing either a pre-heated iron bar or hot water for its purpose. In one type, the bar was placed in an inner section outside which the gravy circulated, and in another the gravy was surrounded by an outer hollow space holding the water. Many argylls resemble tea or coffee pots and do not reveal their use at a first glance.

ASPARAGUS SERVER

It is known that the Romans esteemed asparagus as a vegetable, and it is not unlikely that they introduced it into England. In the

Pocket apple-corer by Joseph Willmore, Birmingham, 1819. Length open 10.8 cm, closed 6.5 cm.

seventeenth century it was still being enjoyed: Mrs Evelyn, wife of the diarist, was given some that had been grown at Battersea, her husband praising it for its flavour; this he considered superior to that of the imported Dutch variety which was raised with the aid of manure. His contemporary, Samuel Pepys, also mentioned the delicacy. On 20 April 1677 he noted: 'So home; and having brought home with me from Fanchurch-street a hundred of sparrowgrass, cost 18*d*, we had them and a little bit of salmon which my wife had a mind to, cost 3*s*; so to supper . . .'. We do not know how either Evelyn or Pepys served their asparagus; there are no records of anything devised then to assist in transferring the stalks from dish to plate. From the late eighteenth century there were tongs, of which the type most often seen are like large-sized sugar tongs with a sliding fitment to stop the ribbed blades from springing too far apart.

BADGE

Badges made of silver were worn for ornament and identification, forming part of the uniform of such diverse groups as the Yeomen of the Guard and employees of insurance companies, City Company servants and many others. The lengthy list would include the arm-badge worn by the winner of the annual race for six Thames watermen instituted by the actor and theatre-manager Thomas Doggett. He awarded a coat and badge for competition in honour of the accession of George I in 1716, the badge bearing a representation of the White Horse of Hanover and the word LIBERTY. Doggett bequeathed money for the continuation of the race each year. Ceremonial badges were worn also by Freemasons and members of other societies.

Badge by Hester Bateman, 1776. 14 × 12.5 cm. *Phillips.* It was worn on the coat sleeve of an employee of the Hand-in-Hand Fire Office

BASKET

Silver baskets to contain bread, cake or fruit were pierced and modelled to appear like wickerwork. The earliest example recorded is dated 1597 and is circular without handles, but by *c.* 1700 it was usual for the basket to be oval with a small handle at each end. A few decades later, the

Basket by Peter Archambo, 1736. Length 31.1 cm. *Sotheby, King and Chasemore*

handle was usually hinged at each side and was bent across the top of the basket, and by the close of the eighteenth century end handles re-appeared. A variation of the foregoing type was in the form of a large scallop shell with the upper part of the sides pierced in a fancy pattern and with a fixed handle curving above.

John Hervey, later first Earl of Bristol, purchased a basket on 7 October 1696, noting in his diary: 'Paid James Seamer yᵉ goldsmiths man Thomas Outlaw for yᵉ great silver chased baskett, weighing 128 ounces, 4 dwt., at 5s. 5d. per ounce, £34.10.0.'
The average weight of a basket was about 60 oz, occasionally rising to 80 oz, so the Hervey example merited the owner's adjective 'great'. *See* Sweetmeat basket.

BATON
See Military and naval plate

BEAKER
The beaker is a simple drinking vessel with a long ancestry. An English silver one dating to as far back as 1496 is recorded, but the majority of survivors are no older than the seventeenth century. In shape the beaker is tall, slightly tapering from the base upwards, with a spreading mouth and often a moulded shallow band round the base. Decoration was frequently sparse, being confined in many instances to engraved ornament and a coat of arms or crest, but some specimens were chased. The beaker was by no means exclusive to England, similar vessels being made in the Netherlands, Scandinavia and elsewhere. Sets of beakers, each nesting one within another sometimes with a cover for the topmost, exist but are rare, and pairs that fit mouth-to-mouth for travelling are sometimes to be seen.

BELL
A small tall-handled bell was often the central fitting of an inkstand, placed conveniently to summon a servant for taking a letter. Many of the bells have been parted from their inkstands and have long led a separate existence, although it is equally possible that they started life on their own. An example of the reverse process occurred in 1741 when the Goldsmiths' Company commissioned Paul de Lamerie to make an inkstand to incorporate a bell that had been presented to them in 1666 by Sir Robert Vyner.

The earliest known example is hall-marked 1636, but Michael Clayton points out that a noticeable proportion of bells of the kind bear no marks despite their liability to be assayed normally. Most of the bells were of plain pattern with one or more bands of raised moulding round the body and a baluster handle. Larger table-bells of similar appearance are comparatively scarce, and rarer still are spherical examples of the kind once used on horses' harness. Bells were sometimes awarded as prizes at race meetings, giving rise to the expression 'to bear away the bell' applied to a winner.

An unusual use of bells occurred at coronations, at which a canopy was held over the sovereign by Barons of the Cinque Ports. The number of the latter involved varied from occasion to occasion: at the coronation of George III in 1761 a report of the procession from

Beaker, maker's mark E G in an oblong shield, 1678. Height 23 cm. *Phillips*

Westminster Hall to the Abbey stated that the King and Queen each walked beneath a canopy of cloth of gold borne by 16 Barons. The canopies were supported on staves, to each of which was attached a silver bell that was claimed by the bearer as a perquisite. A few of the bells have survived and it is noticeable how they varied in design: the simplicity of one used at George I's ceremony

Bleeding bowl by James Rood, 1711. Diameter 24 cm. *Sotheby Bearne*

contrasting with the intricate pattern of those made for the crowning of George IV in 1821.

BELLOWS *See* Chimney furniture

BIGGIN *See* Coffee pot

BLEEDING BOWL
The name given to a shallow bowl *c.* 12 cm in diameter, with a single flat pierced handle. It has been argued that they were made for use as porringers, caudle cups, or as wine tasters. To complicate matters, American collectors call them porringers, and Charles Oman re-printed a seventeenth-century English reference to them under that name. He quoted from an advertisement for lost plate in the *London Gazette* of 20 October 1679 which included '3 Porringers (one with the ear off)'. The fact that in 1689 a surgeon is recorded as ordering such a bowl does not prove that he used it in blood-letting; he may equally have eaten from it.

BODKIN
Old silver bodkins used for threading ribbon, laces and so forth have survived, but being small and light in weight they were seldom marked. An exception is one stamped with the initials S P, which are probably those of Samuel Pemberton, a Birmingham maker of small wares who was active from *c.* 1784. It measures 6.5 cm in length. An earlier specimen is 15.2 cm long, has a tiny circular spoonlike wax-holder at the top and is pricked with initials and the date 1692. A cylindrical or oval small case for bodkins was often attached to a chatelaine.

BOOKBINDING
Paul Hentzner, a German visitor to London in the 1590s, noted seeing at Whitehall books bound in coloured velvet 'with clasps of gold and silver'. In the following century Samuel Pepys wrote in his diary for 2 November 1660:
'In the afternoon I went forth and saw some silver bosses put upon my new Bible, which cost me 6s–6d the making and 7s. 6d the silver; which with 9s–6d the book, comes in all to 1–3–6 my Bible in all. From thence with Mr. Cooke, that made them, and Mr. Stephens the silversmith to the tavern and did

Bowl by William Hamilton, Dublin, 1723. Diameter 24 cm. *Bonhams*

give them a pint of wine.'
Silver used in bookbinding was usually confined to Bibles and the Book of Common Prayer. The practice was seldom successful: if chased sheets were used as panels on the sides damage was difficult to avoid, and heavy sheets endangered the hinges. Pepys followed the more practical method of applied studs or bosses, although they prevented a volume from being stored on a shelf without harming its neighbours. Incidentally, his Bible is not among the books in his library that is now at Magdalene College, Cambridge.

BOSUN'S WHISTLE
The boatswain's name derives from 'boat' and 'swain', the latter meaning servant, the word being pronounced as it is now written: 'bosun'. He was a naval warrant officer in charge of sails, rigging

and much else in his ship, and in a merchant vessel held the post of foreman. The bosun summoned his men by whistle, and some of the surviving examples are of silver. They date from the eighteenth and nineteenth centuries and some bear bright-cut engraved decoration.

BOUGIE BOX *See* Taper box

BOWL
A bowl is described as a drinking vessel, the term being applied to one with or without a foot and optionally with a cover and/or a matching dish or stand. The earliest recorded English example is the Studley bowl and cover of the 1380s in the Victoria and Albert Museum. There are later specimens of all dates and for a variety of purposes, not all of which relate to potable liquids. In fact a bowl had, and still has, innumerable uses and it may be said that it defies precise definition. *See* Mazer, Monteith, Punch bowl, Quaich, Sugar bowl and basin.

BOX
Silver boxes were made for many purposes: to hold a variety of specific articles or simply to contain odds and ends. In the accounts of Sir Thomas Myddleton, 2nd Baronet, of Chirk Castle, there is an entry dated June 1667 reading:
'pᵈ at Shrewsbury assizes, for a small silver box for the barronett, to keep small money iijs. vijd. . . .'
It was an unusual container for his petty cash.
   In the nineteenth century elaborately designed silver and silver-gilt boxes, or caskets as they were termed, were made to hold presentation addresses. Although today it is often impossible to be certain of the intended use of a box, others are more easily classified. *See* Counter box, Seal box, Snuff box, Soap box, Spice box, Tobacco box, Toilet service, Vinaigrette.

BROOM (Hearth brush)
See Chimney furniture

BUCKLE
Buckles were favoured as a fastening for several articles of clothing from hats to shoes. In the eighteenth century they were often made of silver, but many had the tongue of steel with the precious metal reserved for the decorative portion. They varied in shape and size according to both function and fashion. Shoe buckles were especially the target of changing taste; in 1734 a dandy being described as wearing pumps with 'fine wrought buckles as big as those of a coach-horse, covering his instep and half his foot'. Thirty years later they remained sizeable, the Rev. William Cole making this clear when he wrote in his diary for 26 January 1767:
'I gave Tom [his servant] and Jem leave to go to see the Montabank at Fenny-Stratford, & gave each of them with Sarah something to try their Luck at the Lottery. Jem & Sarah who went Shares got a large Pair of Silver Buckles.'
By the late 1770s they had expanded yet again, and in the 1790s went out of fashion altogether. Some men who specialised in their production in London were listed in the *Universal British Directory* of 1790:
'William Eley, Patent silver buckle mftry., 14 Clerkenwell Green
Joel Jacobson, Silversmith & buckle maker with patent springs, 37 Charles Street, Hatton Street
Thomas Kirkham, Silver buckle maker, Monkwell Street'

BUTTER CONTAINER
Some butter containers were of silver with pierced and decorated sides and glass liners, others clearly stated their purpose by having on the cover a seated cow that served as a handle. A further variety, lidless, was in the form of a scallop shell; they are referred to as 'butter shells' but equally they may have been used at the table for pickles or sweetmeats. All the foregoing appeared in the last quarter of the eighteenth century, often accompanied by butter knives with handles of mother-of-pearl or ivory and curved blades.

BUTTON
Silver buttons were made in the eighteenth and nineteenth

Butter pail by J H, Greenock, c. 1800. Width *c.* 15 cm.

centuries and earlier. They were in sizes to conform with the clothing to which they were attached: thus, a waistcoat had smaller buttons than a coat, the former being termed 'breast buttons'. Coat buttons attained a noteworthy diameter around 1775, when they were remarked on as being 'large to excess'. Most of the buttons were decorated with chased, stamped or engraved designs that catered for all tastes. The liveried employees in a great house wore buttons bearing their employer's crest or arms, and hunt servants were similarly distinguished. In the early decades of the nineteenth century silver buttons embellished with sporting subjects enjoyed popularity, many sets being supplied by the bookseller, bookbinder and printseller, Thomas Gosden, who catered for the interests of the Fancy. In 1821 he published *Impressions of a series of Animals, Birds, &c. from a Set of Silver Buttons relative to the Sports of the Field*, engraved by J. Scott after drawings by A. Cooper. Buttons are only occasionally hall-marked in full, but if made after 1790 they should have been submitted for assay in the normal manner if weighing over 5 dwt apiece.

CADDINET *See* Ceremonial plate

CADDY SPOON

Short-handled spoons for ladling tea from a caddy came into use in the 1770s, the majority of them emanating from Birmingham. Their

Caddy spoon by George Unite, Birmingham, 1865. Length 7.7 cm. *Sotheby's Belgravia.* It is in the shape of an eagle's head and wing

design varied widely; many of them being oval-bowled like a miniature ladle and decorated with bright-cut engraving. Others were cast or stamped in the shape of a jockey's cap, a salmon or a bird's wing. The foregoing are scarce examples, and along with others have been faked to supply eager collectors.

CANDELABRUM and CANDLESTICK

Candelabrum The candelabrum, a candlestick for more than one light, was known from the fourteenth century. More modern mentions occur in the late 1600s, when they are usually referred to as branches or branch-candlesticks. Candelabra followed the design of table candlesticks, with their branches swirling or stiffly severe according to prevailing taste. It is not unknown to find that a branch was added to a normal

candlestick and bears a date letter different from the latter, and there are other instances in which a branch of Sheffield plate was provided for a silver candlestick. The tall candelabra popular on early nineteenth-century dining tables were commented on unfavourably by Dr William Kitchiner. He suggested that they 'seem intended to illuminate the Ceiling, rather than to give light on the Plates, &c.'. In his opinion there should be about half as many candles as guests, and the flames should be *c.* 46 cm above the table.

Table Candlestick The number of silver candlesticks surviving from before 1660 is surprisingly small in view of the probability that they must have been numerous. Extant examples of mid-seventeenth century date are similar to brass and pottery ones of the time, with a wide spreading trumpet-shaped foot, central broad greasepan and a narrow greasepan at the top. Candlesticks of similar appearance were made in the

Netherlands, whence originated also the design of many of the specimens made after 1660. All followed a trend towards lowering the central greasepan and widening the upper one so that the former duly became merely ornamental, and the base was flattened. A popular design was in the shape of an architectural column; a theme that re-appeared 100 years later. By 1700 French influence began to show, with the earlier central pan becoming even slighter and dropping to near the base, and with alterations in detail in conformity with changing styles this set the outline for several decades. There was no lack of inventiveness, with some makers adapting a human figure as a stem, and others exploiting rococo, Gothic and Oriental

Candelabra

(*below*) by Edward Feline, 1743; branch by Jonathan Alleine, 1768. Silver-gilt, height 36.3 cm
(*right*) by Matthew Boulton, Birmingham, 1824. Height 69.3 cm. *Christie's*

motifs. The earlier candlesticks
were hammered from sheet
metal, but from about 1670 they
were cast, often in separate parts
that were soldered together.

Hand or Chamber Candlestick The
candlestick comprising a socket
in a shallow tray with a handle is
well-known in all metals, not
least in silver. One was
mentioned in a document in
1438, but any dating to before
1700 are rare. Surviving
specimens of all dates vary in
details of design and ornament.
Some of the late
eighteenth-century examples
have a rectangular space under
the socket to hold a pair of
snuffers, and provision for a
'dunce's cap' extinguisher to slot
into the handle.

Hanging Candlestick In October 1689
John Hervey bought 'a silver
hanging candlestick for the
nursery, weighing 17 ownces, 10
pennyweight, £5.11.0.' What it
looked like can only be guessed,
but presumably it held a single
candle and hung where it was
out of the reach of children.

Library Candlestick This has a heavy
base from which rises a vertical
rod on which slides an adjustable
holder for one or two candles, the
glare from them being controlled
by a movable shade. Pepys was
given one, 'done in silver, very
neat', in 1669, but examples in
the metal of any date are rare.

Taperstick The taperstick held a
candle of small diameter and its
purpose was to melt the wax

Table candlesticks (*opposite page*)
(a) maker's mark R B with a crescent and
pellets below, 1674. Height 14.3 cm.
Christie's
(b) by John Quantock, 1756. Height
24 cm. *Phillips*
(c) probably by James Gould, 1725.
Height 16 cm. *Sotheby, King and
Chasemore*
(d) by David Marshall, Edinburgh, 1768.
Height 30.5 cm. *Sotheby's*
(e) by Henry Hobdell, 1777. Height
32 cm. *Woolley and Wallis, Salisbury*
(f) by Samuel Whitford, 1819. Height
19 cm. *Sotheby's*
(g) by William Elliott, 1814. Height
28.5 cm. *Sotheby's*
(h) by John Watson, Sheffield, 1835.
Height c. 26 cm. *King and Chasemore*

Hand candlesticks
(*above*) maker's mark I C with a star
beneath in a heart-shaped shield, 1673.
Diameter 10.7 cm. *Phillips*
(*right*) by Matthew Boulton, Birmingham,
1803. Height 12 cm. *Sotheby's*

(*below*) Wall candlestick or sconce,
maker's mark I S between escallops,
1687. Height 31.7 cm. *Sotheby's*.

used for sealing letters before gummed envelopes came into use. Tapersticks followed the design of full-sized candlesticks, but some formed one of the fittings of an inkstand where they were conveniently placed for sealing letters. They were often complete with an extinguisher that was attached by a short chain. *See* Taper box

Wall Candlestick The wall candlestick, or sconce, was to be found in many large houses from the Restoration onwards. In 1721 the various Royal palaces had more than 200 between them, but the majority have vanished. The earlier examples were of flimsy construction and held a single candle before a shaped back panel that acted as a reflector, but by *c.* 1700 they were being cast and as a result were considerably more substantial. Many bore the arms and crests of Royal and noble owners, some remaining to this day in the possession of their descendants. Not all of the sconces were completely of silver, one kind having mirror backplates: John Hervey noted paying £75 5s for silver borders for '8 glass sconces' in January 1699. From the same silversmith, David Willaume, a month later he bought '8 great silver sconces'

Card case by Frederick Marson, Birmingham, 1850. Height 8.7 cm. *Sotheby's Belgravia*. It bears a relief view of the Crystal Palace

A CARRIAGE-LAMP, contributed by Messrs. HALLMARKE, ALDEBERT, & Co., of London, forms the subject of the annexed engraving. It is made of the finest and most massive glass, beau-

tifully cut and set in silver; it is, altogether, one of the richest and most creditable specimens of such articles we remember to have seen.

Carriage lamp from a woodcut in the *Art-Journal Illustrated Catalogue* of the Great Exhibition, 1851

weighing just short of 500 oz, that cost him £175 inclusive of engraving.

CARD CASE

The conventions of Victorian social life placed an emphasis on the paying of formal visits and the exchange of cards, carefully engraved in copperplate lettering with the name, and sometimes also the address, of the caller. Suitable silver cases in which to carry the cards were made so that they remained in pristine state until they were presented. The cases were ornamented with chased, stamped or engraved decoration, rectangular in shape, measuring *c.* 10 by 7 cm by a few mm thick with the lid hinged. Popular subjects on them

were views of well-known buildings, or landmarks such as the Scott Memorial in Edinburgh.

CARRIAGE LAMP

The pairs of lamps on town carriages were as decorative as they were functional, the most ornate examples combining the sparkle of cut-glass with the shine of polished silver. One such that was displayed at the Great Exhibition in 1851 was described in the *Art Journal* as 'one of the richest and most creditable specimens of such articles we remember to have seen'. Another, shown by Benjamin Black of South Molton Street, London, bore national emblems, the Royal arms and St George and the dragon, as well as being surmounted by a dove holding in its beak an olive branch.

CASTER

The still-familiar article with a perforated top from which sugar and spices can be sprinkled, or cast, has a lengthy history. From the seventeenth century onwards they were often made in sets of three; one of them being blind (unpierced) and intended for powdered mustard, which was generally used in that form until the 1750s. The casters of the 1660s were usually cylindrical with domed tops, often referred to as 'lighthouse' shape. Square and octagonal examples are known, but are comparatively rare. The lids were held in place in various ways, sometimes by means of a bayonet joint similar to that used with English electric light bulbs, but more often a simple push fit was employed and occasionally the lids were hinged. During the course of the eighteenth century the shape changed to a baluster on a pedestal foot, and with minor variations from time to time this remained popular until *c.* 1810. From then onwards there was an increasing liking for bird and animal forms that were modelled realistically and often gilt.

CAUDLE CUP

During the fifty years each side of 1700 caudle was a popular beverage variously compounded of broth, milk, wine and eggs, given to convalescents and others. The caudle cup is generally accepted to be a two-handled cup, with or without a cover and stand, the cup itself being pear-shaped and with chased ornament. On 7 December 1698 John Hervey noted his purchase of 'a chafin dish with a cawdle-heater', showing that the liquid might be taken hot. This is borne out in old recipes, one of 1742 for Flummery Caudle, a mixture of fine oatmeal with wine and eggs, concluding with the words 'Drink it hot for a breakfast'. Some of the cups were given a tall curved spout through which, presumably, the contents were sucked or poured, and these are often termed posset pots or spout pots on the assumption that they were made to hold posset. This was always very different from caudle, being made from milk curdled with wine and

Casters
(*left*) by Jonathan Stocker and Edward Peacock, 1706. Height 15.2 cm *Sotheby, King and Chasemore*
(*right*) by Paul de Lamerie, 1724. Height 22.8 cm. *Christie's*

Caudle cup by Walter Scott, Edinburgh, 1707. Height 31.1 cm. *Christie's*

ale and sometimes with the addition of eggs and cream. The porringer is not dissimilar in appearance to the first-named, and there is no lack of disagreement over the correct designations of all three vessels.

CENTREPIECE *See* Epergne

CEREMONIAL PLATE
The most significant ceremonial plate is that used during the coronation of the sovereign. The majority is of gold and outside the scope of this book, but one article meriting a mention is the silver-gilt caddinet, an article that originated in France where it was known as a *cadenas*. It is a rectangular tray with two lidded compartments of different sizes raised across one of the narrower ends. The larger compartment was to contain a knife, fork and spoon, the small was for salt and a napkin rested on the tray. In France use of the cadenas was confined to royalty and a few other persons, and it is thought that it had been seen in use

there by the exiled Charles II who introduced one for his coronation. That example has vanished, but the two used at the coronation banquet of William and Mary on 11 April 1689 may be seen in the Jewel House at the Tower of London.

Such objects as maces and oars, chains of office, swords of State and staves of office survive in the possession of public and other bodies. Many are still displayed on important occasions and retain a consequence dating back in time. The mace, for example, acquired its significance in the mid-thirteenth century, gaining its name and form from the iron war mace used in battle. The maces of the Royal bodyguard, the serjeants-at-arms, kept in the Tower of London, are of silver-gilt and date variously from the reigns of Charles II, James II, William and Mary and Queen Anne. The most historic English mace is that denoting the authority of the Speaker of the House of Commons, which dates from 1649, the time of the Commonwealth, when it bore non-regal symbols that were subsequently replaced by emblems of Royalty.

A more modern and mundane item of ceremonial silverware is the trowel that was so often presented to whoever laid the foundation stone of a building. Like the silver-bladed spade that was the reward on other occasions, the trowel was engraved with an inscription recording its use. Likewise, a silver or gilt key was usually earned by the person who declared open a completed edifice.

CHAFING DISH

A chafing dish was a bowl-like stand holding burning charcoal, on which was stood a dish or plate to be kept heated. Pepys ordered one on 10 January 1666, and just thirty years later John Hervey paid James Seamer 6/6d an oz for one weighing 24 oz 15 dwt: about £8.00. He bought a heavier one in 1698, 'a chafin dish with a cawdle-heater', weighing 51 oz 18 dwt, paying James Chambers 5/6d an oz or about £14.00 for it. Chafing dishes continued to be popular until the mid-eighteenth century.

CHAIN *See* Ceremonial plate

CHAMBER POT

John Hervey, who had recently been ennobled as Earl of Bristol, bought a chamber pot weighing 30 oz in 1714 and had his insignia engraved on it. Among the Corporation plate at York is a chamber pot of 1670, and in the same county a mayor of Leeds is said to have owned one for use when travelling in his coach. This last example was made in 1818 by Robert Garrard, and is fitted with a lid and two handles that give it a resemblance to a tureen.

CHANDELIER

Silver chandeliers were too costly to have been commonplace. A few have escaped the melting-pot, unlike one of *c.* 1630 that was thus disposed of in Moscow in 1814. A chandelier at Colonial Williamsburg, Virginia, was made for William III in 1695, and probably sold from the Royal Collection by order of George III in 1808: this was the occasion when the Prince Regent urgently needed money for furnishing the apartments of his estranged wife. A few other old chandeliers are known, their numbers including two of 1735 by Paul de Lamerie in the Kremlin, Moscow; one of *c.* 1690 at Hampton Court Palace; and one of 1752 belonging to the Fishmongers' Company hanging in their Thames-side Hall.

CHATELAINE

A series of short chains hanging from a hook that was itself attached to the belt of a robe was termed a chatelaine. It was worn by the industrious housewife, enabling her to have at hand such necessities as keys, sewing aids and so forth. The chatelaine was fashionable during most of the eighteenth century, and there was a limited revival of its use in Victorian times.

CHEESE SCOOP

Scoops for serving cheese had silver curved blades and date from the late-eighteenth century. Some later examples were fitted with a simple mechanism, worked by the user's thumb, to push the cheese off the scoop and on to the plate.

CHEESE STAND

Stands designed to hold a circular cheese on its side so that a wedge can be cut from it are not uncommonly found, made of mahogany and dating from the late-eighteenth century. In 1760 the 9th Earl of Exeter purchased one of silver, which must have proved satisfactory as he acquired another four years later. The earlier of the two is now in the Victoria and Albert Museum.

CHESS SET

The origins of chess reach back into antiquity. King Solomon, a Chinese Emperor and Aristotle have all been suggested by different authorities as originating the game. It would seem to have been played in England by at least the twelfth century, and in view of this it is perhaps surprising to learn that the earliest surviving English silver set dates from the reign of Charles II. Two others of later make are recorded: one of *c.* 1750 and another of 1816. The sides are differentiated by one being of silver-gilt and the other of plain silver.

CHIMNEY FURNITURE

Andiron Andirons, often referred to as firedogs, were used in pairs in the great open fireplaces before coal came into use for heating the home. They supported the logs and allowed access of air so that they burned satisfactorily. Each was made of iron, sometimes ornamented with brass or surmounted by a bronze figure and rarely were decorated with silver. This last was principally in the form of chased sheet metal over the iron core. Most such andirons have disappeared, including those noted in his diary for 24 January 1690 by John Hervey:

'Paid for a pair of silver andirons for my dear wife her closett chimney, £13. 5. 0.'
and on 31 December 1697:
'Paid Watt Compton goldsmith in Lincoln's Inn ffields for 2 pair of Andirons & 2 little knobbs for tongs & shovel weighing 307 ounces 14 dwtt. at 5s. 4d. per ounce, £82. 1. 0.'
Examples survive in a number of mansions including Ham House,

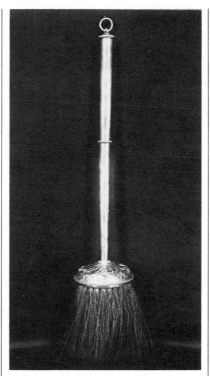

Chimney furniture
(*left*) Andiron, *c.* 1680. Height 48 cm.
Sotheby's
Bellows and hearth-brush, *c.* 1675. *Ham House (Victoria and Albert Museum)*

Richmond, where they have remained continuously since *c.* 1675.

Bellows A pair of bellows was an indispensable fireside accessory, and while most were plainly functional others were decorated. Some bore on their sides panels of silver. When Horace Walpole paid a visit to Ham House in 1770 he noted 'silver dogs, pokers, bellows, &c., without end. One pair of bellows is of filigree'. They had been listed in an inventory of 1688 as being 'garnished with philogreen'.

Broom A broom or hearth-brush to keep the area about the fireplace free of ash would be mounted in silver to match other accessories.

An example at Ham House was listed in 1677 when it was provided with a silver hook from which to hang it.

Fire-irons A pair of tongs, a shovel and usually also a poker were part of the equipment of the fireplace, some of those at Ham House being noted as 'garnisht with silver'. The ornamentation was, of course, limited to the handles.

Fire Screen A tripod-based fire screen made of iron with silver mounts is at Ham House and can be dated *c.* 1675. It is probably the one listed in 1679 and 1683 as 'One screen with Screen Stick garnished with Silver'. Screens of similar pattern, with an adjustable sliding panel, are more familiar in mahogany dating from the mid-eighteenth century.

Hearth Rod The hearth rod was a metal rod forming a slightly raised division between the front and back of a fireplace. Its purpose was to keep ash from spreading and keep the area neat and safe. At Ham House the seventeenth-century inventories recorded hearth rods made of silver.

CHOCOLATE POT
In June 1657 readers of the *Public Advertiser* were informed that they could drink chocolate at 'bishopsgate, in Queen's Head Alley, at a Frenchman's house', and no doubt trendy Londoners flocked there. The earliest surviving pot for serving the beverage is hall-marked 1685, and like some others of pre-1700 date is of tall tapering cylindrical shape with a domed cover, closely resembling coffee pots of the time. A few others had bulbous bodies and flatter bun-like covers, later examples favouring that form. In one particular they differ from coffee pots: chocolate, which was a thicker form of modern cocoa, would remain as sediment in the pot if it was not stirred before pouring. For that reason a small opening was provided in the top of the cover through which a stirring-rod or molionet could be introduced. This orifice was given a lid of its own, either hinged or sliding, and its

Chocolate pot by Isaac Dighton, 1704. Height *c.* 25 cm. *Parke-Bernet Galleries*

presence is positive evidence that a pot was intended for chocolate and not for coffee. Chocolate pots were rarely made after the 1740s.

Chocolate pot by John Elston, Exeter, 1707. Height 18.8 cm. *Royal Albert Memorial Museum, Exeter*

CLARET JUG
In the nineteenth century it became customary to serve claret at the table from covered jugs. A proportion of them were completely of silver, but especially in later years many were of glass in mounts of silver or silver-gilt. The glass vessel was clear or frosted, with or without cutting, and varied from clear to coloured. Shapes were no less the subject of inventiveness, some of the jugs taking the form of birds with humorous expressions.

COFFEE POT
As was the case with chocolate and tea, coffee was introduced into England in the seventeenth century. Its use spread from Arabia to the Near East, and after coffee houses had opened in Constantinople (now Istanbul) and Venice they were soon appearing in the west. Despite an enemy of the bean terming it 'a base, black, thick, nasty bitter, stinking Puddle Water' the public coffee house became established in London. The serving of it in the home soon followed. The oldest surviving silver coffee pot, hall-marked 1681, was presented to the East India Company, and was no doubt for the use of the Directors of the concern. Notably the handle was placed at a right-angle to the spout; the body being of a tall tapering cylindrical shape that remained popular, with variations, for about fifty years. Changes in design involved the body sometimes being faceted while retaining its tapered outline, and the occasional appearance of a 'tucked-in' base: the latter curving inwards and then outwards to form a low spreading foot. By 1750 the shape had become bulbous and twenty years later the foot was made taller. During the nineteenth century there were revivals of the older shapes.

A rival to the coffee pot in its simple form appeared on the market by c. 1800. It was the cylindrical coffee biggin with an integral strainer, stand and lamp,

Claret jugs. All *Sotheby Bearne*
(*left*) by Robert Harper, 1880. Engraved clear glass, height 30 cm
(*centre*) by Charles Reily and George Storer, 1841. Faceted green glass, height 28.5 cm
(*right*) by W. and G. Sissons, Sheffield, 1885. Silver-gilt with engraved clear glass, height 26.5 cm.

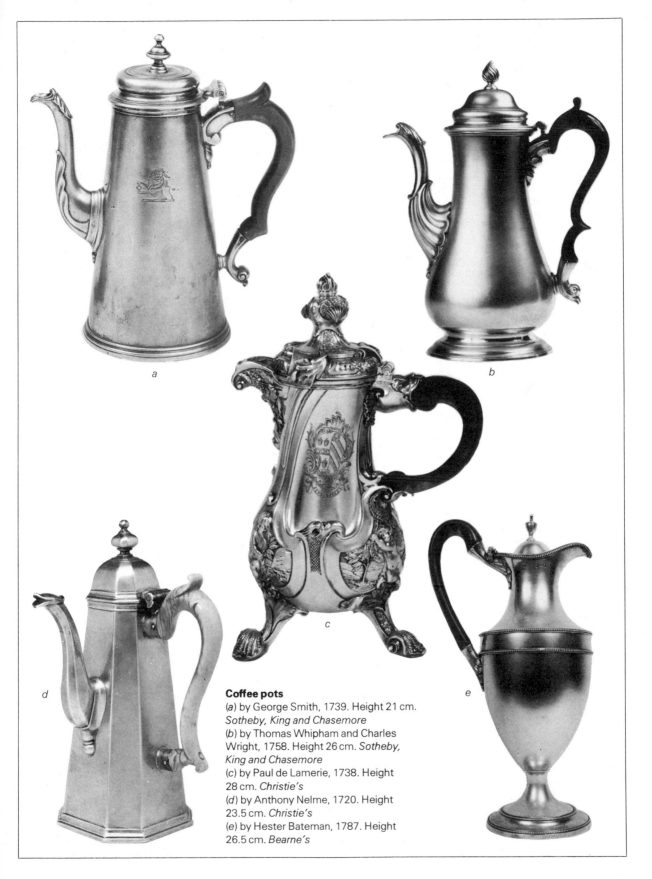

Coffee pots
(a) by George Smith, 1739. Height 21 cm.
Sotheby, King and Chasemore
(b) by Thomas Whipham and Charles
Wright, 1758. Height 26 cm. *Sotheby,
King and Chasemore*
(c) by Paul de Lamerie, 1738. Height
28 cm. *Christie's*
(d) by Anthony Nelme, 1720. Height
23.5 cm. *Christie's*
(e) by Hester Bateman, 1787. Height
26.5 cm. *Bearne's*

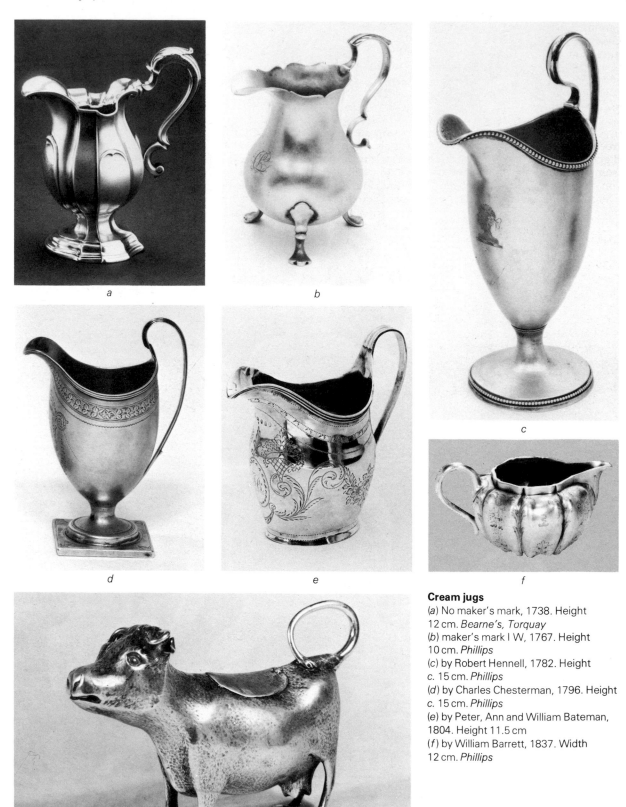

Cream jugs
(a) No maker's mark, 1738. Height
12 cm. *Bearne's, Torquay*
(b) maker's mark I W, 1767. Height
10 cm. *Phillips*
(c) by Robert Hennell, 1782. Height
c. 15 cm. *Phillips*
(d) by Charles Chesterman, 1796. Height
c. 15 cm. *Phillips*
(e) by Peter, Ann and William Bateman,
1804. Height 11.5 cm
(f) by William Barrett, 1837. Width
12 cm. *Phillips*

Left
Cream jug by John Schuppe, 1756.
Length 16 cm. *Phillips*

gaining its name from its inventor, George Biggin. He was described in his obituary printed in the *Gentleman's Magazine* of November 1803 as 'a gentleman of considerable literary and scientific acquirements', who spent much of his time at Woburn Abbey investigating the barks of various trees for use in tanning. 'Mr. Biggin', recorded the *Magazine*, 'some years ago, invented a new sort of coffee-pot, which has been ever since extensively manufactured'.

COMB BOX *See* Toilet service

CORKSCREW
Corks began to be used as bottle closures during the seventeenth century, replacing waxed cloth wrapped round a wooden plug. At first the cork was tied with string or wire to hold it in place, but then an anonymous genius thought of driving in the cork flush with the rim of the neck and providing a corkscrew, sometimes known as a bottle screw, to remove it. In the nineteenth century much time was spent devising trouble-free corkscrews that did not overtax the strength of the user. While the screw itself was made of steel, the more extravagant examples were given silver mounts.

CORONET
When John Hervey was created Earl of Bristol he noted in his diary in 1714: 'Oct. 19. Paid Louis Cuny for my Earls Coronet, £14'. Cuny, who was a Huguenot immigrant, had premises in Panton Street, Haymarket. In contrast to the price of the coronet, the legal and other charges in connection with the earldom amounted to £395 18s 7d.

COUNTER BOX
Small cylindrical silver lidded boxes containing gambling counters survive from the seventeenth century. Each contains up to thirty thin silver discs bearing Royal likenesses. An exceptional and earlier example in the Victoria and Albert Museum contains 39 Elizabethan sixpenny pieces that are contemporary with it.

CREAM BOAT *See* Sauce boat

CREAM JUG
The small jug accompanying a teapot, whether it holds milk or cream, is usually termed a cream jug and in the United States is known as a creamer. In the mid-seventeenth century, when knowledge of the Chinese habit of tea-drinking spread in the West, it was also known that in the Orient it was taken with a little milk. The habit was slow in becoming general in England, and as late as 1698 Lady Russel wrote to her daughter that she had lately 'met with little bottles to pour milk out for tea'. Presumably she was referring to jugs of some kind, but none made prior to a decade later has been recorded. The shapes of the jugs varied over the years, fashion dictating that they followed prevailing styles. Standing apart from fashion were the novel and surprising jugs that were made mostly by John Schuppe, who registered his mark in 1753. His jugs are modelled as an open-mouthed cow, the curled tail forming a handle and the hinged cover in the back of the animal sometimes with a large-scale fly to serve as a knob.

CREAM PAIL
Cream was sometimes brought to the table in a silver open-topped vessel simulating a wooden pail with brass hoops and a swing handle. Examples date from *c.* 1730. Forty years later they were made raised on a foot, often with pierced sides and a glass liner, but these may also have served as sugar basins.

CRUET
A cruet is a set of bottles and small ewers for condiments contained in a frame. The article dates from *c.* 1710 when the various components were made of silver, but towards the end of the century silver-mounted cut-glass bottles, etc, were used. The frames ranged in shape from cinquefoil at the start to boat-shape in the early 1800s. At some time in the nineteenth century the frame was often termed a Warwick, apparently because of an erroneous belief that an Earl of that name owned the earliest example.

CUCUMBER SLICER
This handy and unusual piece of tableware was first made in *c.* 1770. An example sold at auction in 1982 was described in detail: 'A silver-mounted bone cucumber slicer, of oblong spatula form with lug handle, the detachable blade held at a slight angle against bone supports by two bolts with wing terminals, the salient points of the bone body with stepped silver rivets, 22.2 cm. (8¾ in.) long.' The blade bore the makers' mark of Peter and Jonathan Bateman, but was without a date letter so could only be described as '*c.* 1790'.

CUP
The cup, usually with a matching cover, has for long been an esteemed article of silverware. Much care has been lavished on its

Cup and cover (standing cup), maker's mark I E with three pellets below, 1598. Silver-gilt, height 43.2 cm. *Sotheby's*

Cup, cover and stand (racing trophy) by
William Holmes and Nicholas Dumee,
1774. Height 54.6 cm. *Leeds City Art
Galleries*

design and production, and the
regard in which cups have been
held is demonstrated by the
numbers that have been preserved
down the ages. The earliest
specimen, the 'King John Cup',
belonging to the Corporation of
King's Lynn, dates from *c.* 1350,
and many of later dates are extant
to show changing styles. The tall
standing cup was supplanted at the
end of the seventeenth century by
the two-handled cup and cover; an
object that challenged silversmiths
to give of their best. All the great
names were connected with their
production, as were the foremost
designers: William Kent and Robert
Adam being the most successful. In
many instances it is difficult or
impossible to differentiate between
a cup and a vase. *See* Caudle cup,
Lloyd's patriotic fund vase,
Porringer, Vase, Warwick vase,
Wine cup.

DESSERT SERVICE
Services for dessert were made
from the second half of the
eighteenth century, often of
silver-gilt to prevent tarnishing
from contact with food. The plates
and dishes were sometimes
designed appropriately in leaf
shapes with fruit in low relief. A
late example of such a service,
dating from 1880 and now in the
Victoria and Albert Museum, is
enamelled and parcel-gilt and
includes a multi-branched
centrepiece.

DINNER SERVICE
An Irish visitor to London, the
Reverend Thomas Campbell,
remarked in 1775 how very alike
were the dinners served at the
tables of the great: soup, fish and
saddle of mutton, turkey and
pigeons for the second course
followed by a dessert of ices and
fruit. He added that when he had
dinner with the Thrales in
Streatham 'the two first courses
were served in massy plate'. The
third course, dessert, for which
perhaps porcelain was used,
comprised 'four different sorts of
Ices viz. Pineapple, Grape,
raspberry & a fourth'. With so

Dessert bowl by Thomas Heming, 1764.
Width 49.5 cm. *Sotheby, Parke Bernet*

Cups and covers
(*left*) by Edmund Pearce, 1709. Height
24 cm. *Sotheby's*
(*right*) maker's mark I L, Dublin, 1748.
Height 37.5 cm. *Christie's*

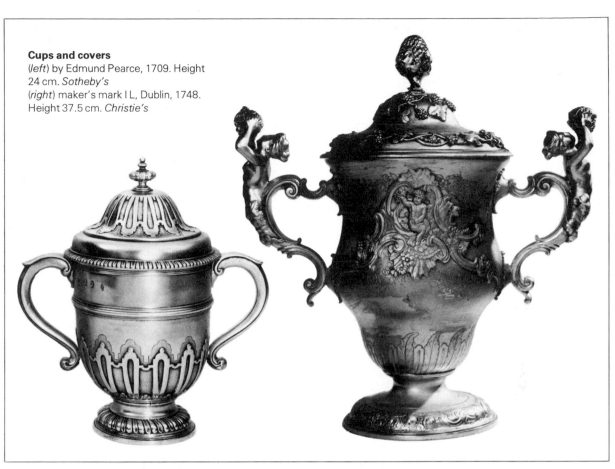

Dish cross by Burrage Davenport, 1774. It adjusts to hold a dish up to 38 cm in width

much food from which to choose it is no wonder that the wealthy owned large services of matching plates and dishes. Ornament on the various items was confined to the borders with the addition of an engraved crest or coat of arms. If the arms were those of Royalty the service was most probably the perquisite of office of a Government official or an ambassador, so-called Ambassadorial Plate. The number of pieces comprising a dinner service varied according to needs and depth of pocket. It is known that the service given by Charles II to the Duchess of Portsmouth in 1672 had 130 plates and dishes of various sizes as well as candlesticks, saltcellars and much else that brought the total weight to 6730 oz. Almost exactly a century later the service supplied to Sir John Cust when he was elected Speaker of the House of Commons included 80 plates and dishes, together with tureens for sauces and soup, candlesticks and a huge wine cistern, the latter weighing 1457 oz.

DISH COVER

Domed covers for meat and other dishes were sometimes of silver, but were more usually made from the late-eighteenth century onwards of Sheffield plate. In order to find a modern use for the covers many have been cut in two and converted into wall lights. Thus

Dish ring by Joseph Jackson, Dublin, c. 1780. Height 9 cm. *Sotheby, King and Chasemore*

treated they tend to look exactly like bisected dish covers.

DISH CROSS

The dish cross supplanted the chafing dish. The most popular type of cross comprised two hinged arms forming an X and fitted with a central heater. It could be adjusted with ease to fit any size of dish. A few dish crosses date from the 1730s, but their use did not become general for a further twenty years.

DISH RING

This was used to raise a dish of hot food from contact with the table, saving the surface of the latter from damage. A few English silver rings are known, but the majority were made in Ireland between c. 1750–1820. They were chased and pierced with ornament that varies in pattern as does the diameter and height of the rings. They are sometimes named as potato rings, and it is not unlikely that some were employed to support a dish or bowl of the vegetable.

DISH WEDGE

These were used to tip up one end of a serving dish so that any liquid gathered at the opposite end could be retrieved without trouble. The top surface of the wedge was serrated or beaded to give it a purchase and some of them had ring handles. Most examples date from the years 1790–1810.

DOG COLLAR

In 1707 the Chirk Castle accounts recorded:
'March 24 p^d Mrs Anne Moore, wch she laid out for a silver coller for Mr Wm Myddelton's little dog x^s'
A few earlier examples are extant, but most are of later date. It is not improbable that the collar

Opposite page
Seven-light candelabrum by Robert and Sebastian Garrard, 1856. Height 98 cm. *Arne Bruun Rasmussen, Copenhagen.* It is modelled with St George slaying the Dragon, and was presented by Queen Victoria to Baron de Plessen, Danish Minister at St Petersburg (Leningrad), 'in grateful recognition of important services rendered to British subjects 1854–56'.
See page 84

presented to Frederick, Prince of Wales by Alexander Pope would have been made of silver. On it was engraved the couplet penned by the donor:

I am his Highness' dog at Kew;
Pray tell me, sir, whose dog are you?

DOUTER and EXTINGUISHER

To dout meant to extinguish and was a form of the expression 'do out'. A douter was of scissors form, closely resembling sugar-nippers but with flat-surfaced grips. They were usable with candles, and would have been effective in reaching the wicks of heaters under kettles and other vessels. A conical extinguisher often accompanied a hand-candlestick, which had a small square slot for its reception; the extinguisher was given an angled lug to fit the slot. Alternatively the tray had a raised cone on which the extinguisher rested.

Opposite page (see also page 119)
Standing salt, 'The Vyvyan Salt', maker's mark W H with a flower (?), 1592. Silver-gilt inset with panels of painted glass, height 40 cm. *Victoria and Albert Museum: photo, Bridgeman Art Library.* The subjects of the panels are from *A Choice of Emblemes, and other Devises* ... by Geoffrey Whitney, published in 1586; a book known to Shakespeare.

DRESSING CASE *See* Toilet service

ECUELLE

As its name suggests, the ecuelle originated in France. It is a shallow covered cup, usually with two flat handles, and is complemented by a matching stand. A few were made in England, in the main by immigrant silversmiths, but the vessel did not affect the popularity of the caudle cup or the porringer.

EGG BOILER

This was a vessel to hold the water standing above a heater, usually with an hour-glass rising from the lid, and sometimes with egg cups and spoons in places provided for them. The whole apparatus was a highly practical device for cooking one or more eggs to suit the personal taste of a breakfast-taker, who was enabled to serve himself at whatever hour he chose to leave his bedroom. Egg boilers were made from *c.* 1800. An entry in John Hervey's diary, in the handwriting of his wife and dated 3 February 1690, notes that she had been given a 'silver ege thing worth tenn ginnes', and it may be wondered if this is a reference to an egg boiler.

EGG CUP and FRAME

Silver egg cups with gilt interiors were made from early in the

Ecuelle and cover by Pierre Harache, *c.* 1690. Silver-gilt, diameter 12.8 cm. *Christie's.* The inscription records that it was presented as a christening gift in 1690

---

eighteenth century. They were generally accommodated in a frame that held up to eight cups and there were places for an appropriate number of spoons. Some frames had a centrally-placed glass salt cellar. The earliest recorded example dates from 1740.

ENTREE DISH

The entrée is defined as a 'made' dish; one composed of several ingredients such as a hash or a ragout, served before the main course of a dinner. It was contained in a shallow covered dish, often with two handles and raised on a stand holding a heater. The dishes came in sets, and while in the 1750s their shape was a matter of taste, from *c.* 1800 they were usually oblong.

EPAULETTE

See Military and naval plate

EPERGNE

The epergne served a decorative purpose as an attractive central ornament on the dining table, and at the same time held candles, or

casters, or small dishes with sweetmeats and savouries. A report of the Lord Mayor's banquet held at the Guildhall, London, on 9 November 1761 mentioned that between the courses of the meal there was placed on the table at which were seated George III and Queen Charlotte 'a grand silver epergne, filled with various kinds of shell fish of different colours'.

One of the earliest examples was listed in 1721 as being in the Jewel Office in Whitehall. It was described as a gilt 'aparn' with four salt boxes, four small salts, four candle-arms, six casters and four sauceboats, with a total weight of 783 oz. Another, of 1741, in the Hermitage, Leningrad, was made by Augustin Courtauld and is comparably equipped, with the base raised on feet formed as dolphins and the dishes and candle-nozzles supported on ivy-entwined snakes. Epergnes made between *c.* 1740–60 take full advantage of the prevalent rococo style, many of them incorporating Chinese elements such as pagoda roofs hung with small bells and a plentiful use of rockwork and leafy branches. In due course they were being made to conform to the plainer lines of the neo-classical, while Paul Storr and his contemporaries produced epergnes in the style of their day with Egyptian and other motifs then

Epergne by William Cripps but also marked by John Jacobs, 1755 and 1756. Height 52 cm. *Christie's*

current. Epergnes dating from after *c.* 1800 are often referred to as centrepieces.

ETUI
The etui or etwee was a container for small implements, and was most often of tapered shape with a hinged lid. The contents varied according to the sex of the owner: a lady would have a bodkin, pair of tweezers, ivory memorandum tablets, pencil holder, scissors and so forth, a man would have a folding ruler, penknife and other requirements. Etuis were worn suspended from a chatelaine and were popular during the second half of the eighteenth century.

EWER and **BASIN**
In the days before forks were in use it was an essential mealtime ritual for a diner to clean his fingers from time to time. This was performed with the aid of a ewer containing scented water that was poured into a basin for the purpose. The articles were of silver or silver-gilt, surviving examples dating back to the early sixteenth century. Their

Right
Epergne or centrepiece perhaps by Philip Cornman, 1806. Height 47 cm. *Sotheby's*

(*above*) Pair of ewers and basin by
Benjamin Pyne, 1699. Silver-gilt,
diameter of basin 61.6 cm. *Christie's.*
The engraving is noteworthy

(*left*) Pair of ewers by Pierre Harache,
1697. Silver-gilt, height 23.5 cm. *Leeds
City Art Galleries*

production continued for a
considerable time after the
introduction of forks, but the ewers
and basins were then made as
decoration for the sideboard rather
than to fulfil their original role.
Some of the smaller examples may
once have formed part of toilet
services.

EXTINGUISHER *See* Douter

FIRE-IRON *See* Chimney furniture

FISH SERVER
Slices intended for serving fish
came into use during the second

half of the eighteenth century. Most of them clearly proclaim their use by their design, which incorporated one or more pierced and engraved fish. Many were given silver handles that were generally made by a specialist maker, not necessarily by the man who made the blade. By the 1800s handles were most often of ivory and in due course each slice was sold with an accompanying fork of more or less matching pattern. The knife with blade ending in a blunted point for eating fish, paired with a fork, was a nineteenth-century innovation.

FIRE PAN (grate)
See Chimney furniture

FIRE SCREEN
See Chimney furniture

FLAGON
Flagons, or livery pots, like many other items of plate suffered from changes in definition over the years. During the reign of Elizabeth I the flagon was a bottle or flask usually having a length of chain attached to serve as a handle, and what was termed a pot or livery pot was a lidded vessel resembling a tall tankard. In the first quarter of the seventeenth century the latter began to be called pots, but fifty years later what had earlier been known as flagons were also being called pots. Charles Oman decided to clarify the position by terming a bottle a flagon, and a tall tankard a livery pot; which he did when describing the English silver in the Kremlin, where a number of important examples are displayed. The articles, which had been presented to the reigning Tsars by leaders of British embassies in the years 1557–1663, had been preserved there with care, completely forgotten and unknown to English antiquaries until casually mentioned by a newly-arrived Danish ambassador to London in 1880. Comparable pieces in England are, or were, almost exclusively to be found in churches, where they contained the communion wine; their presence

(*right*) Ewer by Hunt and Roskell, 1876. Silver-gilt, height 38 cm. *Phillips*

Flagon, maker's mark a goose in a dotted circle, 1687. Height 22.8 cm. *Sotheby's*.

emphasising the difficulty in many instances of differentiating between ecclesiastical and secular plate.

FLASK

Pocket flasks, with or without a detachable cup, were carried at outdoor events where their contents would prove welcome. An Irish example of *c.* 1690 is recorded, as is one made in Edinburgh in 1751. There are also some surviving English flasks of eighteenth-century date, but the majority of extant ones are Victorian and later.

FORK

Forks were used very occasionally in England in the sixteenth century, and there is an isolated mention of one in a will of 1463. There it was termed 'my silvir forke for grene gyngor', and fifty years later another was described as being used for the same delicacy. It was not until the 1600s that the fork was employed to supplement the knife when dining. The best-known reference to what was then a novelty appears in *Coryat's Crudities*, published in 1611, in which Thomas Coryat tells of his five months of travelling on the mainland of Europe. He wrote: 'I observed a custome in all those Italian Cities and Townes through which I passed, that is not used in any other country that I saw in my travels, neither doe I think that any other nation of Christendome doth use it, but only Italy. The Italian, and most other strangers that are cormorant in Italy, doe alwaies, at their meales, use a little forke when they cut the meate . . .'

Coryat explained that the Italians were fastidious, disliking meat on a dish being touched with the fingers, 'seeing all men's fingers are not alike cleane'. Slightly earlier, the playright Ben Jonson had referred to the subject in his comedy *Volpone*, first acted in 1606, in which one of the characters says: 'Then must you learn the use and handling of your silver fork at meals'. Pepys noted on 14 December 1664 that he ordered some spoons and forks, and from about that date their use was increasingly general. However, as much as a century later at least one man felt embarrassed by them. Joseph Brasbridge, who had a retail silversmith's business in Fleet Street from 1770, wrote about an invitation to dinner he received from one of his customers. The meal was to be enjoyed at a fashionable hotel 'where the cloth was laid with a profusion of plate', but Brasbridge could not do justice to the occasion. In his own words, ' "because" said I, taking up one of the silver forks, "I know how to sell these articles, but not how to use them".'

The earliest known English fork is one in the Victoria and Albert Museum, it is hall-marked 1632 and has two prongs and a flat stem of rectangular section with an indented top. Three-pronged forks were made from *c.* 1680, four-pronged became widely accepted about 80 years later, but on the whole it is unwise to date examples by the number of tines as these were a matter of personal choice. Steel-tined forks were usual from *c.* 1750, some of them with handles of cast silver, but many of thin sheet metal stamped with a pattern. Both kinds were produced in two halves which were soldered together, the latter being filled with composition to give them strength.

FURNITURE
A few pieces of furniture made principally of silver or of wood covered with decorated sheets of the metal were recorded as existing prior to the Restoration. Thenceforward for a few decades it became fashionable among those who could afford its cost, and were happy to contribute to the prevailing ostentation. This was remarked on by John Evelyn, in particular, after visiting the home of the Countess of Arlington in April 1673, when he noted the luxuriousness of her dressing room. He had seldom seen the like: 'to this excesse of superfluity were we now Arriv'd, & that not onely at Court, but almost universaly, even to wantonesse, & profusion'. Surviving examples of this use, or mis-use, of silver are rare, the greatest number in England being in the Royal Collection. Among them is a table and looking-glass at Windsor Castle, presented in *c.* 1690 to William III by the City of London. Such articles were constructed of wood or iron or both, but in this instance castings of solid silver were employed, and in an inventory taken in 1721 the total weight is given as no less than 7306 oz. Of earlier date are a table at Knole, Kent, and another at Windsor that had been a gift to Charles II. Sheet silver was used on a small scale to decorate tables and other pieces, some well-known examples being at Ham House. A table there is of ebony with contrasting chased and pierced mounts on the top, and two writing-cabinets or 'scriptors' of kingwood are similarly embellished.

The first half of the eighteenth century saw the occasional production of tea-kettle stands. Each had a tripod base, shaped stem and the top in the form of a tray or as a ring in which the kettle rested; the former closely resembling more familiar mahogany examples.

GOBLET
A goblet may be defined as being smaller in size than a standing cup and of larger capacity than a wine cup, but like both was supported

Goblet, maker's mark AB conjoined, 1605. Height 17.7 cm. *Sotheby's*

on a stem. Some were given to churches for use as communion cups and it is not always easy to determine if some specimens were made originally for religious or secular use. Pairs and sets of goblets became popular during the second half of the eighteenth century.

GORGET
See Military and naval plate

HEARTH ROD
See Chimney furniture

HONEY POT
Towards the close of the eighteenth century a pot or jar specifically for honey took the form of a skep: a dome-shaped beehive made from straw that remained in use until it was finally supplanted by the wooden hive developed in Victorian times. Some of the silver and silver-gilt skep-shaped pots were given appropriately a bee as a knob for removing the upper half when the lower held the honey. In other instances the honey was held in a glass vessel, and the whole skep was raised to reveal it. The pots were usually complete with a stand having a matching border simulating a bound coil of straw.

HOUR GLASS
Silver-cased hour glasses are known to have existed in the sixteenth and seventeenth centuries, but apparently none survive. Small-sized examples of later date were perhaps for use at the table to time the cooking of a breakfast egg, and some egg boilers were fitted with them.

HURLING BALL
The Cornish game of hurling originated in medieval times, and remains an annual event in two towns: St Columb Major and St Ives. The ball is made from two hemispheres of sheet silver pinned to a turned wooden core, usually of apple-wood, and has an overall diameter of *c.* 7 cm. A number of old examples have been preserved, each exhibiting clear signs of the rough handling received in the boisterous game. They are of nineteenth-century date, but an exception is a seventeenth-century specimen engraved with the words: *Play fare be merry and wise That your sport noe harm arise God save the King.*

INKSTAND
The inkstand, or standish, has existed since the early seventeenth century, but examples made before 1650 are very few in number. Like later ones, the majority of them had places for pens and for three containers: one each for ink, wafers and pounce. Wafers were used for sealing letters before envelopes were introduced; pounce or sand

a

b

c

d

Inkstands

(a) by Philip Rollos, 1716. Length
32.4 cm. *Christie's.* It is engraved with
the arms of George I

(b) maker's mark A I, 1639. Length
42 cm. *Christie's.* It is in the style of
Christian van Vianen

(c) by John Edwards, 1744. Length
42 cm. *Christie's*

(d) by E. and J. Barnard, 1849. Length
41 cm. *Sotheby, King and Chasemore*

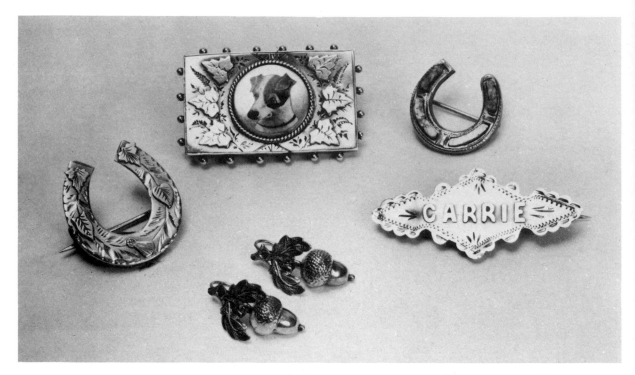

Jewellery (*clockwise from top*) brooch inset with an enamel painting of a terrier's head; maker's mark M E L, Birmingham, 1888. 2.5×4 cm. Brooch inset with coloured stones, maker's mark G H P in a shamrock, 1909. Brooch lettered CARRIE in relief, maker's mark W B, Chester, 1901. Pair of acorn ear-rings, unmarked. Horseshoe-shaped brooch, maker's mark B and M, Birmingham, 1876

was powdered gum sandarach or cuttle-fish used for drying ink prior to the invention of blotting paper and to prevent ink running where an erasure had been made on paper or parchment. The pounce pot had a pierced lid, and the wafer box a hinged one, but in some instances it was replaced by a handbell or a container for lead shot with which to clean a pen. A type of inkstand popular from *c.* 1670 took the form of an oblong casket with two centrally-hinged lids that concealed the fittings; it is sometimes described as a 'Treasury' inkstand. From early in the eighteenth century the article was frequently a shaped rectangular tray raised on short feet with the fittings readily accessible on top, these duly being made of cut glass with silver mounts. From time to time silversmiths incorporated current decorative features and

occasionally devised fresh types. One of the more ingenious of these was in the shape of a globe on a pedestal, half of the upper hemisphere sliding inside the fixed half to reveal the inkpot and other containers.

JEWELLERY

Silver jewellery became very popular as the price of the metal fell following the arrival on the market of ample American and Australian supplies. A further fillip was given when the duty on manufactured goods was removed from 1 May 1890. Much of the jewellery was made in Birmingham, the city having for long been a centre for the production of small items like vinaigrettes and small wares of all kinds; the same techniques, stamping and soldering and engraving, were equally applicable to ornamental brooches and similar items. The variety of their design was endless, ranging from the name of the recipient in letters entwined with ivy leaves to more general good wishes conveyed by the word Mizpah. Others show a horse shoe with or without GOOD LUCK or bear appropriate symbols in commemoration of Queen Victoria's Jubilee of 1897. Silver was fashionable from the 1880s for

chains, necklaces, lockets and ear-rings, as well as for bracelets, and in all these also there was a continual succession of novel designs to tempt buyers.

JUG

Jugs of all shapes and sizes have been made of silver; their uses were no less varied. There has been confusion over the centuries between ewers, flagons and what were termed in old inventories 'livery potts', and it is not always clear as to what was meant. Pairs of large-sized jugs, some with their handles engraved A and B, were intended for serving ale and beer at the table. Others would have been designed to hold hot liquids, and would originally have had their handles insulated with a covering of woven wicker that has often worn out in use and has not been replaced. Smaller-sized lidded jugs dating from *c.* 1750 are often thought to have been used for hot water but may well have held coffee. Others, akin to cream jugs in size, but with lids, may have been intended for hot milk. In the first decades of the nineteenth

Opposite page
Jug by Phillips Garden, 1754. Height 34.3 cm. *Sotheby's*

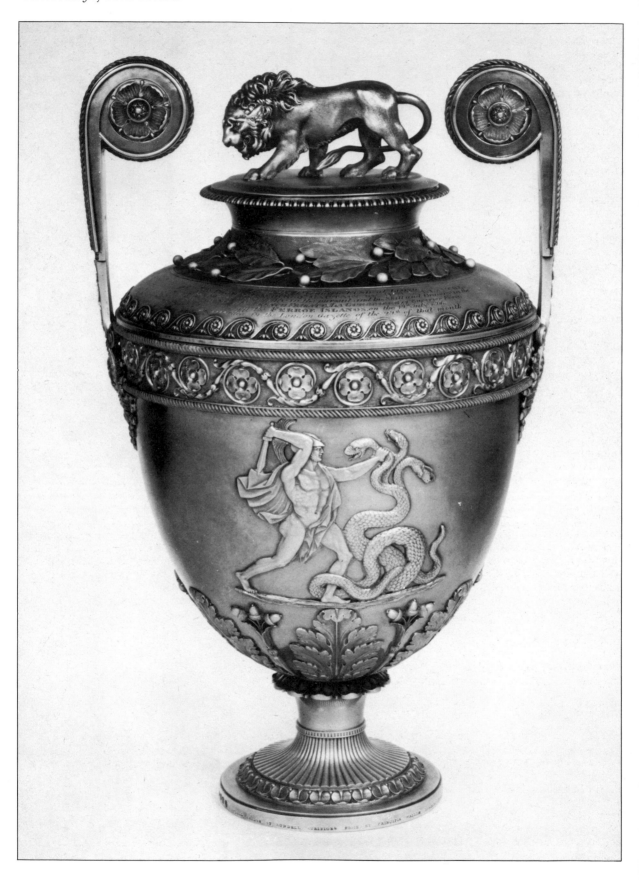

century some fine jugs for hot water, complete with stands and heaters, were supplied by Rundell, Bridge and Rundell. Their makers included Paul Storr, who also produced some jugs of classical form for less obvious uses.

KNIFE

The steel-bladed knife was sometimes given a silver handle. This was cast or stamped in two halves that were soldered together, and the latter type was filled with a composition to give it strength. The most popular shape was like a pistol butt, the blade with an incurved back and rounded end. Dessert knives likewise had silver handles, the better ones with silver blades gilt to prevent tarnishing from contact with fruit juice. Fish knives, which appeared during the nineteenth century, were sometimes given silver blades that were pointed to facilitate dealing with bones.

LADLE

Ladles for serving stews and similar dishes were perhaps the large-bowled spoons with long tubular handles that are described nowadays as basting spoons. The more familiar type of ladle has a pear-shaped, round or oval bowl set at an angle to the curved handle. It dates from *c.* 1720 and was used, according to its size, with soup and sauce tureens, and with sauce boats, in all cases occasionally of matching design. By *c.* 1760 ladles formed part of a suite of tableware and were supplied as a component along with knives, forks and spoons. *See* Caddy spoon, Punch ladle.

LANCER'S CLOAK CLASP
See Military and naval plate

LIVERY POT *See* Flagon

Opposite page
Lloyd's Patriotic Fund vase by Digby Scott and Benjamin Smith, 1805. Height 38.7 cm. *Huntington Art Gallery, California: photograph, Christie's.* Presented to Captain Thomas Lavie of HMS *Blanche* for his skill and bravery in capturing a French frigate on 19 July 1806

LLOYD'S PATRIOTIC FUND VASE

Members of Lloyds, the London insurers, decided in 1803 to open a general subscription for the establishment of a Patriotic Fund. It was to reward those 'who may be engaged in the Defense of the Country, and who may suffer in the Common Cause . . .', and realising that many of those meriting awards might be offended by a gift of cash, it was proposed that a vase or a sword would prove worthy substitutes. The vase would be the most important of the two, and was designed by John Flaxman after the prize-winning design of a recently-qualified architect, John Shaw. It was based on a classical shape, with a figure of Britannia on one side and on the other a warrior slaying a serpent above the words BRITONS STRIKE HOME. The order for supplying the vases went to Rundell, Bridge and Rundell, with their actual manufacture being the work of Smith and Scott and Paul Storr. Together they produced 73 vases of which 66 were presented, leaving seven not awarded. The average vase cost £100, but others were less expensive, and Nelson's widow, his brother, and Admiral Collingwood received vases valued at £500 apiece.

MARROW SCOOP

Marrow, the soft white substance found in the cavities of some bones was a favoured delicacy, and is still prized in parts of the country. Boiled marrow-bones were served at the table, so that diners could enjoy their contents with toast. Alternatively, according to a recipe printed in 1705, the marrow was encased in puff pastry together with a mixture of herbs, currants, egg-yolks and sugar. To extract the marrow from the bones when served in the first-noted manner silversmiths provided special scoops, which were of three kinds. The most common had a grooved channel at each end, one of greater width than the other, with a central section left plain or faceted forming a 'handle'. A rarer type was in the form of a spoon of which the handle terminated in a scoop. Rarest of all was a fork with a similar handle, of which only a

single specimen of *c.* 1670 has been recorded. The other varieties were made from the late seventeenth century onwards.

MAZARINE

A mazarine was at one time a deep plate or dish used for serving a ragout: a kind of stew. In this connection Andrew Marvell wrote in 1673 '. . . what Ragouts had here been for you to have furnish'd the Mazarines on your Table!' Over a century later, in 1796, readers of *The Art of Cookery* by Mrs Hannah Glasse (the lady wrongly credited with instructing a cook to 'First catch your hare') were told to use a mazarine for serving Water Tansey: a custard-like dish requiring a dozen eggs, various flavourings, spinach juice, and 'one small sprig of tansey'. Norman Penzer suggested that mazarine was a diminutive of mazer; a vessel that would be suitable for serving a ragout or even water tansey. The modern use of the word applies it to a pierced fish-strainer, usually oval but occasionally circular, that fits into a dish and allows any liquid to drain away from the contents.

MEDICAL INSTRUMENTS

Silver was used for making a variety of medical instruments, especially during the nineteenth century. A proportion bears neither a maker's name nor a hall-mark, so dating can only be approximate. It relies largely on a knowledge of the period in which a particular item was current, but a number are inscribed with the name of an inventor or patentee that can provide a useful clue. The range of professional items includes such things as cases for sets of lancets, tongue depressors, dental mirrors, and tracheotomy tubes. For personal use there were nipple shields, medicine spoons, eyebaths, ear trumpets, spectacle frames, and sets comprising a toothbrush, box for dentifrice and a tongue scraper. In most instances the design of the articles was severely functional, and wherever contact with liquids was likely the surface was gilt.

MILITARY and NAVAL PLATE

Some items of military equipment,

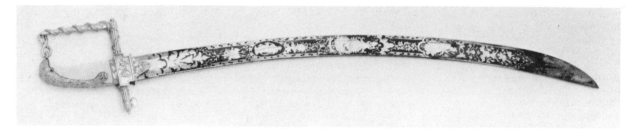

Sword and scabbard by R. Teed, Sword Cutler. Length of blade 76 cm. *Phillips.* Awarded by Lloyd's Patriotic Fund to Lieutenant James Bower of HMS *La Loire* for 'a truly gallant exploit' on 27 July 1803

particularly for full-dress wear, were of silver. Most are scarce, either because they were made in small numbers or were discarded because they were out of date. The articles include:

Epaulette These shoulder ornaments were usually made of gold or silver-gilt thread (bullion), but a late eighteenth-century silver example is recorded.

Gorget A crescent-shaped plate engraved or applied with the Royal Arms or a regimental insignia. The gorget was a relic of steel armour, the silver version being worn similarly at the throat.

Lancer's Cloak Clasp An early nineteenth-century example was described as being formed by 'a cinquefoil and a shaped oval cartouche with wrigglework engraved borders, joined by two chains with "arrow" terminals'.

Shoulder-belt Plate This kept in place the crossed shoulder-belts worn by a soldier, the engraved silver plate resting centrally on the chest of the wearer.

Sword Hilt Silver sword hilts survive from the first half of the seventeenth century. Distinct from its military and naval usage, the sword was part of a gentleman's dress and subject to changes in fashion in the same way as clothing. It was not unusual for a blade to be fitted with one or more hilts in the course of a lifetime. In 1715 Dudley Ryder, later Attorney-General, noted in his diary that he had been 'to buy a sword, which I did, a silver-gilt one for £3. 4s. without the blade.

My old one came to 4½ ounces of silver, which made £1. 4s. 4d. at 5s. 6d. per ounce'. Swords with suitably inscribed and decorated hilts were occasionally presented to military and naval personnel for acts of valour. Lloyd's Patriotic Fund awarded some, and following the Battle of Trafalgar others were given by the City of London. These last were received by Vice-Admiral Lord Collingwood, Rear-Admiral the Earl of Northesk, and Captain T. M. Hardy of *Victory. See* Bosun's whistle, Lloyd's patriotic fund vase.

MINIATURE WARES

Toy-sized wares were popular from *c.* 1680–1750, and have also survived from other dates. It is hard to determine whether some of them were not silversmith's samples, made to show the prowess of the maker and to gain him orders for the real thing. Others may have been produced to furnish the dolls' houses of pampered youngsters. The range of extant pieces is a wide

Monteith by William Gamble, 1701. Diameter 33 cm. *Christie's.* The later engraved arms are those of George IV as Prince of Wales

one, with everything from candlesticks to coffee pots, caddies to casters, and tankards to teapots.

MOLINET
A molinet, sometimes spelt molionet, was the stirrer inserted through the subsidiary lid of a chocolate pot in order to stir the contents. Examples are very rare; one that has survived has a wooden rod fitted at one end with four pierced silver flanges.

MONTEITH
The monteith is a large bowl, about the same size as a punch bowl, but with a notched rim. Filled with cold water, it served to chill glasses that were placed bowl inwards and

---

Mustard pots
(a) by Robert Sharp, 1790. Height 16 cm. *Sotheby's, Pulborough.* It is engraved with the Prince of Wales' feathers within the Garter motto surmounted by the Royal crown, and was donated by Her Majesty the Queen to be sold in aid of Chichester Cathedral Trust
(b) by John Denziloe, 1793. Height 8 cm. *Phillips*
(c) by Peter, Ann and William Bateman, 1803. Length 8.5 cm
(d) by E. and J. Barnard, 1856. Height *c.* 8 cm. *Phillips*

a

c

immersed with their feet in the notches. The seventeenth-century writer, Anthony à Wood, in a much-reprinted anecdote, recorded that the vessel was named after a Scotsman named Monteigh who 'wore the bottome of his cloake or coate so notched'. His fame earned him an ill-rhyming couplet from the pen of William King in *The Art of Cookery*, published in 1708:
New Things produce new Words,
* and thus Monteith*
Has, by one vessel, saved his Name
* from Death.*
The earliest recorded monteith is hall-marked 1684, and they were produced in decreasing numbers for the ensuing hundred years. Georgina Lee noted 261 examples made up to and including 1710, and only 64 between 1711 and 1789. There were two kinds of monteith: those made in one piece, and the others with the rims detachable so that they could serve as punch bowls if required. The majority were chased, many bore engraved decoration, and the heavier ones had applied cast ornament and a pair of loose-ring handles. They ranged in weight from *c.* 30 to 175 oz and in diameter from *c.* 26 to 40 cm.

b

d

MOTE SKIMMER *See* Spoon

MUG
A mug might be defined as a lidless tankard, but this is not always so because a few examples are known with detachable covers. Others, with wide mouths and sloping sides are perhaps described more aptly as cups, but there is often a very thin line dividing one vessel from another. The forms of mugs varied from the straight-sided and tapering to pear-shaped, and decoration tended to be sparse as was suited to a utilitarian object. A small-sized mug was a fashionable

Mug by Solomon Hougham, 1814. Height *c.* 8 cm. *Phillips*

---

christening gift in the nineteenth century, when it became subject to elaborately chased and engraved ornament.

MUSTARD POT
The condiment has a history reaching back into classical times, when Hippocrates used it in medicine. In more modern days the housewife would have purchased the seeds, grinding them in a mortar, and in the sixteenth century its best-known source was mentioned by Shakespeare in *Henry IV, Part II*: 'His wit is as thick as Tewkesbury mustard'. In *c.* 1720 a Mrs Clements of Durham prepared a finer and better-looking product ready for use that she named, predictably, Durham Mustard. It attracted the attention and approval of George I and the lady thereby earned a small niche in culinary history. The condiment was used in its dry powdered state

and it is assumed that the third caster in a set, the one that was unpierced, was used to contain it at the table. The earliest recorded covered mustard pots of familiar type date from *c.* 1725 and their production increased continually thereafter. The 1770s saw the round and oval varieties with pierced sides and blue glass liners that echo the neo-classical style. Many of the nineteenth-century silversmiths let their imaginations run riot, producing pots in unending variety. Especially popular were those modelled as monkeys, owls and other fauna, their presence providing a touch of humour in the dining room.

NAPKIN RING

Apart from a few examples of *c.* 1830, the napkin ring is a Victorian and later addition to the repertoire of articles made of silver. It is found in many shapes, decorated with chasing and/or engraving.

NUT CRACKER

Silver nut crackers are uncommon, doubtless because the metal is not strong enough for the purpose. The earliest variety, of which a small number of *c.* 1700 date survive, are of thumbscrew type: they take the form of a ring to encircle the nut, with a short threaded rod to crack it. Of later period are others hinged at the top, enabling the user to squeeze the shell until it breaks.

NUTMEG GRATER

The hard oval fruit of the nutmeg tree was known to Chaucer who

Nut cracker, *c.* 1720. Height 6.7 cm.
Sotheby's, Torquay

mentioned its use in flavouring ale. Following the Portuguese discovery of the Spice Islands (now Maluku Islands, Indonesia) in 1512 it began to reach Europe in greater quantities and became widely used. Following the Restoration and the introduction of punch, it was found that the addition to the drink of some grated nutmeg improved its

taste; at the same time the spice gave it a slightly soporific effect and increased the action of the alcohol. It became customary for men to carry in a pocket their own nutmeg, and for the purpose silversmiths made a suitable container combined with a small grater. In that way each user had spice that was freshly ground without losing any of its flavour. A pre-1700 form was in the shape of a pierced tube that allowed some of the smell of the nutmeg to escape, perhaps to repel disease. These are not dissimilar in function and appearance to pocket snuff graters in which a plug of tobacco was carried and might have served also as a prophylactic. Later nutmeg graters resembled snuff boxes and others were ingeniously hinged to conceal the grater, which was at first made of silver, punched to roughen the surface, and then of steel. In a few instances the grater was combined with a corkscrew, leaving no doubt that the purpose of the container was to hold a nutmeg.

PAP BOAT

The pap boat was shaped like a footless and handle-less sauceboat and was used to feed a child with a mixture of bread and milk or a similar semi-liquid. The vessel was made from *c.* 1710 until the early decades of the nineteenth century. It was not an especially scarce article, and when they went out of use many were converted into small-sized sauceboats that are superficially attractive while falling into the category of fakes. The majority of pap boats were

Nutmeg grater by Hester Bateman, 1787. Length closed 8 cm. It is shown open for use and closed for carrying in the pocket

hall-marked on the rim at the wide end opposite the spout, so a small sauceboat stamped there should be viewed with due caution.

PATCH BOX

A patch was a small piece of silk or court plaster worn by a lady on the face either as a contrast to the pallidity and softness of the skin or to conceal a blemish. Small boxes, circular or shaped, are often termed patch boxes whatever may have been their original purpose. A distinguishing feature of the true patch box is said to be the presence of a mirror inside the lid so the patch might be applied accurately.

PEN

A silver-cased fountain pen was known in France in the 1650s, when it was reported that everyone who had heard of the novelty wanted to own one. It was perhaps a pen of this kind that was given to Pepys on 5 August 1663, and that he noted using four days later: '. . . I begun to make use of the Silver pen (mr. Coventry did give mee) . . .' Alternatively he may have received a penner.

PENCIL

Cased pencils existed in the eighteenth century, their presence being proved by the exemption from duty of 'Sliding Pencils' and 'Pencil Cases' in the Act that came into force in 1740. The propelling pencil was a mid-Victorian

---

Opium pipe by Thomas Phipps and Edward Robinson, 1808. Length 28 cm. *Phillips*

innovation that owed its success to the improved skills of Birmingham manufacturers. One of them, J. Sheldon of Hampton Street, Birmingham, and Bucklersbury, London, described and illustrated in the 1851 Great Exhibition *Catalogue* one of his more complex pencils. Made in gold or silver, it contained within an engraved casing 'an ever-pointed pencil, penholder, toothpick, half-sovereign gauge, a letter and coin balance'. Soon after that date the firm of Sampson Mordan and Co., of London, became prominent as makers of propelling pencils and other novelties.

PENNER

The penner was a portable container for short quill pens and ink, mostly made in the seventeenth century. The tubular case was *c*. 14 cm in length and one end was sometimes engraved to be used as a seal.

PERFUME BURNER

In the early seventeenth century the perfume burner was a round or otherwise shaped container with a pierced top, the whole raised above a heater. Herbs, spices and resins were used to produce the desired scent, which would make the atmosphere pleasing and might keep germs at bay. The pastille, compounded of a mixture of gum arabic, benzoin and charcoal, would seem to have been introduced into England in the late eighteenth century. Returned from a visit to Paris Horace Walpole informed his friend, the Rev.

William Cole, that he had brought back for him a gift of some china '& also some Incense or Pastilles à bruler; which they use in their Churches, & are very agreable to burn, a little at a time, in one's Parlour, immediately after Dinner is removed, to take away the Scent of the Victuals: & it is a Peice [*sic*] of Luxury I learned with him at Paris'. Cole wrote the foregoing in his journal for 7 March 1766, but he did not receive his presents for several months. Mrs Montagu, the London hostess, confirmed Cole's remarks in a letter of 1771 to Matthew Boulton, telling him that she had perfume burners or casolettes, as they were then termed, brought to the table during dessert: they 'drive away the Vapour of soup and all the fulsome savour of dinner'. Silver perfume burners were few in number at all dates; other metals, and later, porcelain, being preferred.

PIPE

William Harrison, the Elizabethan historian, wrote in 1573 of the spread of tobacco-smoking in England. Smokers used, he said, 'an instrument formed like a litle ladell', which is a fair description of pipes of that time and later. They were normally made of baked clay, but a few early silver examples have been recorded. One, unmarked but datable to *c*. 1620, exactly resembles a clay of the time, with a small-sized bowl set at an angle to, and integral with, the long stem. It was tested in 1955 by its then-owner, who reported that 'the result was most satisfactory'.

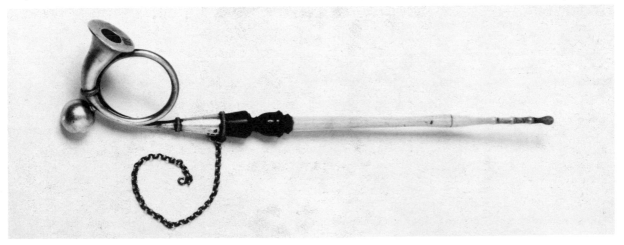

Punch bowl by William Williamson, Dublin, 1751. *Christie's.* It was awarded as a race trophy and is appropriately engraved

PLATEAU
A plateau occupied the centre of a dining table, taking the form of a mirrored glass base on which might stand candelabra and other articles, the whole surrounded by a low gallery. Sometimes a plateau was in a single piece, circular or rectangular, but others were in several sections to run the entire length of a banqueting table. Silver and silver-gilt examples date from *c.* 1800.

PORRINGER *See* Caudle cup

POSSET POT *See* Caudle cup

POSY HOLDER
The posy holder was a Victorian novelty, usually of gilt base-metal but sometimes made of silver or silver-gilt. A typical example of *c.* 1850 was of gilt filigree with a turned and pierced ivory handle, the overall length being 18 cm. Another, also gilt and embellished with split pearls, once belonging to Hannah de Rothschild (later, Countess of Rosebery) had spring-loaded legs that folded for carrying, but when apart formed supports to display its contents. Hall-marked 1873, it was 13 cm in length.

PUNCH BOWL
The word punch is an anglicised form of the Hindustani *panch*, meaning five, and was applied to a popular beverage containing that number of ingredients: spirits, lemons or limes, water, sugar and spices. It was introduced into England during the seventeenth century and became very popular. As the poet Thomas Blacklock wrote:
What harm in drinking can there be,
Since punch and life so well agree?
A bowl of good capacity was necessary for punch-drinking, the average diameter being 30 cm, some examples being complete with a lid to keep the contents warm between servings. The earliest silver bowls date from the 1680s and their production continued into the early decades of the nineteenth century. Some were plain except for a moulded rim and foot, but others were finely engraved or chased or had cast ornament.

PUNCH LADLE
The silver punch ladle had a circular bowl with a tubular handle of the same metal or of wood set at an angle to it. Some examples were made to match the bowl with which they were supplied. Soon after 1750 the handle was often made from a length of whalebone, dark grey in colour and twisted to provide a grip, the base of the silver bowl being inset with a coin.

PURSE
Purses of leather, cloth or needlework were sometimes given silver mounts with hinged sides and a catch at the top. Only a small proportion has survived the vicissitudes of time and use, and they are mostly of nineteenth-century date. Purses of silver chain mesh were more durable, although a later introduction. In 1898 a London retailer listed them at prices between 9s and £1 13s (45p and £1.65) according to size and shape.

QUAICH
The word derives from the Gaelic *cuach*: cup, the quaich taking the form of a shallow vessel made from upright staves, hooped, and with two upstanding handles or ears. They were used in Scotland, and although mostly of wood some silver examples are known. Many of the latter were engraved to simulate wood and they date from the seventeenth century onwards.

RATTLE
In Roman times medicinal and other virtues were attributed to coral, and children wore pieces of it in the form of necklaces to preserve them from danger. Later, an almost indispensable item of a baby's equipment was a rattle combined with a short length of coral, the noise being contributed by small bells. These were of silver or silver-gilt attached to the coral by a mount of the same metal. Rattles of the kind have been known for several centuries, one being shown in a portrait of Edward, Prince of Wales, who was born in 1537 and succeeded to the throne as Edward VI in 1547. An Act passed in 1739 exempted from duty, among other small wares, 'Coral Sockets and Bells', but they were subject to normal treatment from 1790.

RELIGIOUS PLATE
As early as AD 847 it was proclaimed that only precious metals should be employed for making chalices. This edict has been followed with few exceptions to the present day, both for the chalice in use at the Roman Mass, and for the communion cup used in celebrating the Eucharist in the

established churches of England, Scotland, Wales and Ireland, although both vessels are often referred to today as chalices. The chalice disappeared at the Reformation; those not seized by the authorities either being hidden or melted for conversion into communion cups. These were often accompanied by a paten for the Holy bread; the paten usually in the shape of a small dish with a sunken centre, later versions being supported on a short foot. The newly-introduced cup of the 1560s often had a matching paten fitting it as a cover when reversed, the foot then forming a convenient handle for its removal. A design favoured at that time followed the current simple shape of the beaker, with a minimum of ornament apart from a band of engraving. Later, there were more elaborately-embellished cups, but only occasionally was their design of a quality comparable with their workmanship.

For diluting the wine with water in pre-Reformation times the liquids were contained in a pair of ewers, or cruets; one marked V for *vinum*: wine, and the other Λ for *aqua*: water. Their place was duly taken by flagons of greater capacity that were sometimes of baluster shape on a spreading foot, but were more often tall and cylindrical and similarly based.

After the Reformation it was usual for candlesticks to be displayed on the altar. Their larger size distinguished them from secular examples, and many were topped by a spike-like pricket rather than by a nozzle. In most instances the bases are large in order to provide good stability.

The practice of Roman Catholicism was outlawed at the Reformation, but was continued secretly by those who eschewed the established faith. From time to time they required additions to, or replacements for, their altar plate and pieces for the purpose were supplied by English silversmiths.

In *c.* 1830 a re-awakening of religious fervour in the Anglican church and the emancipation of the Roman Catholics were followed a decade later by a powerful Gothic revival. The revival, which affected the contents of churches no less

than their architecture, was led by Augustus Welby Northmore Pugin who strove to recapture in every way the vitality of religion in the Middle Ages. As regards silverware, little or nothing remained from that distant past on which the new Gothic might be modelled, and it required men like Pugin and his followers, who were steeped in the period as much as was possible, to design articles with both aesthetic and ecclesiastical merit. They designed plate for the established church as well as the Roman, the latter requiring a range that included censers, monstrances and ciboriums.

Cromwell, and later the City of London, permitted Jews in England to practise their religion, and the synagogue in Bevis Marks in the City was built between 1699 and 1702. Others followed in the eighteenth century and later. A number of silver articles played a part in Jewish ceremonies, these including the eight-armed Hanukah lamp; the Kiddush cup; the pointer used in reading from the Scroll of the Law; and Rimonim, or finials with bells that decorated the Scroll. In many instances they were supplied by silversmiths who had no affiliations with the Jewish faith.

ROSE BOWL
A silver bowl filled with roses provided a familiar sight and scent in Victorian English homes. Doubtless in many instances out-dated punch bowls were brought from the attic and given a new lease of life, or there were new bowls of similar appearance to be bought. A rose bowl was often a prize at horticultural and other exhibitions and examples are to be seen inscribed to that effect.

SALT and SALT-CELLAR
The standing or ceremonial salt was a piece of plate of considerable social significance in its day. Its position at the table separated the host and principal guests from less important diners, and its magnificence testified to the wealth and power of the establishment. From the Middle Ages down to the middle of the sixteenth century salts were generally of hour-glass

Standing salt, 'The Eddystone Salt', by Peter Rowe, Plymouth, *c.* 1698. Height 48.2 cm. *City Museum & Art Gallery, Plymouth.* This is a contemporary replica of the lighthouse erected on the Eddystone Rocks by Henry Winstanley, and which was destroyed in a storm in 1703

a   b   c

d

Salts
(a) by John Elston, Exeter, 1718. Height 3.6 cm. *Royal Albert Memorial Museum, Exeter*
(b) by Robert Hennell, 1818. Length c. 7 cm. *King and Chasemore*
(c) by Paul Storr, 1814. *Christie's*
(d) by Joseph Craddock and William Reid, 1818. *Phillips*

outline, but at times there were types that diverged from the norm. Designers and silversmiths at all periods gave rein to their imaginations, incorporating pearls, gemstones, rock crystal, panels of painted glass and other extravagances with cast, chased and engraved silver-gilt. The majority of the foregoing were mainly ornamental, with little provision for actually holding salt. For this purpose, each diner would have had next to his plate or trencher, a trencher salt. These were variously shaped, small and squat with a central depression; their decoration, if any, was slight and in marked contrast to that of

the standing salt that, with some exceptions, ceased to be made after c. 1700. Samuel Pepys recorded on 19 June 1665 that he paid £6 14s 6d for a dozen silver salts which came, he added, from his 'little new goldsmith's, whose wife endeed is one of the prettiest modest black [-haired] women that ever I saw'. By c. 1740 the salt began to grow in height by being raised on short feet and was given decorative details in accordance with the styles that succeeded each other in passing decades. They were supplied in multiples of two, from a pair to a

dozen or more. The interiors were gilt to prevent corrosion from the salt, or were fitted with glass liners to the same end.

SALVER and **WAITER**
According to Thomas Blount, writing in 1661, a salver '. . . is a new fashioned peece of wrought plate, broad and flat, with a foot underneath, and is used in giving Beer, or other liquid thing to save the Carpit or Cloathes from drops'. In many instances a salver was made to match a tankard or other vessel, but in the course of time the two articles have become separated. By the early eighteenth century the salver was also known as a 'waiter' and as a 'table', the terms apparently being interchangeable, and at the same time it began to be treated in many instances as a piece for display as much as for utility. The larger examples were found to be particularly suitable for engraving. It became customary, too, to convert out-dated seal matrixes into salvers; examples being immediately recognisable from the engraved representations of the seals whence they originated. The earlier salvers had, as Thomas

Salver by David Willaume, 1720. Diameter 17.7 cm. *Christie's*

Blount stated, 'a foot underneath', which was in the form of a short cylinder with a spreading base, but by *c.* 1720 this was replaced by three or four dwarf feet at the outer edge. The latter was the subject of shapes varying from the plain circular to octafoil and the complex outline known as 'piecrust'. As the century advanced rococo scroll-and-shell flat borders were replaced by upright pierced galleries, and during the Victorian period the earlier styles were revived with variations to suit tastes of the period. *See* Tea table, Tray.

SAUCEBOAT and SAUCE TUREEN

Although the word was apparently not used before *c.* 1750, the sauceboat certainly existed some thirty years earlier. At that date it was a boat-shaped vessel with a prominent lip at each end, a handle at either side and a low pedestal foot. Within ten years an improved type came into use, this had a spout at one end and a handle at the other, with a deep body raised on low feet or a pedestal. It proved more manageable at the table than the double-ended variety and remained the basic form thereafter. Minor differences in design affected the feet, which might be palmate, spade shaped or ball-and-claw; and the handle, which might be a complete leafy scroll or a so-called

'flying scroll' resembling the letter C and open at the front. A proportion were of considerably more ambitious design; for example, with open-mouthed dolphin masks for pouring or with entwined dolphins as supports, possibly for use with oyster or shrimp sauce. From *c.* 1765 open tureens and stands and small tureens on pedestal bases and with covers became fashionable. After

Sauce tureen and cover by John Watson, Sheffield, 1818. Length *c.* 22 cm. *Bonhams*

c. 1800 there was a return to feet as supports and the popular shape was oblong. Many sauceboats were *en suite* with soup tureens, salt cellars and much else, and a large table laid with such a service was a dazzling sight.

a

b

c

d

Sauceboats
(a) by William Shaw, 1730. Length *c.* 21 cm. *Christie's*
(b) by Benjamin Godfrey, 1739. Length 21.5 cm. *Sotheby's*
(c) by Robert Makepeace, Newcastle, 1749. Length 18 cm. *Sotheby Bearne*
(d) by Peter, Ann and William Bateman, 1799. Length 21 cm.

SAUCEPAN

Although silver saucepans are often referred to today as brandy saucepans there is doubt whether many were used to heat that spirit. William Kitchiner told readers of his cookery book to keep a pint-sized pan especially for melting butter, adding in a footnote: 'a silver saucepan is infinitely the best, – you may have one big enough for a moderate family for four or five pounds'. A few seventeenth-century examples exist but most date from the reigns of the Georges. Shapes and sizes vary, as do the handles; which are usually set at right angles to the lip. Some of the pans have engraved decoration, while one of 1787 by Hester Bateman is characteristically given bright-cut engraving and is topped by a hinged lid.

SCIENTIFIC INSTRUMENTS

Scientific instruments were made of silver in small numbers. They include microscopes, among them one partly of the solid metal supplied by George Adams, 'Instrument Maker to His Majesty', for the use of George III; an instrument that has been described as 'the most lavish and least practicable ever devised'. There survive other, less cumbersome, large and small pieces of apparatus. If inscribed at all, they bear most often the name of the dealer in such articles who sold them, sometimes followed by the word *fecit*; which implies that he was the actual maker, but this was rarely correct. Lacking the evidence of his personal mark, the true maker remains anonymous.

SCONCE

See Candlestick (Wall candlestick)

SEAL

A seal, by which authenticity was given to a document bearing it, was impressed in wax by means of a matrix engraved in reverse with a coat of arms or other device. Some of the matrices were of silver, and important ones were broken or otherwise defaced on the death of the sovereign or of the owner. In the former instances the matrix became a perquisite of the holder of an office of State, such as the Lord

Chancellor or the Lord Privy Seal. Sometimes the metal was re-fashioned into a useful or decorative article. Thus in 1574 the Lord Keeper, Sir Nicholas Bacon, who held office on three occasions, had three covered cups made, one for each of his houses. Each was suitably inscribed, one of them now being in the British Museum. Later office-holders also had their outdated seals made into cups, and later again into salvers. Small-sized seals for personal use were made in large numbers, and between *c*. 1740–90 did not have to be hall-marked as they were exempted from assay.

SEAL BOX

From the twelfth century the seal on a document was no longer applied on the parchment, but was attached to it by a strip of parchment or a short length of cord. This practice made it liable to be damaged, so for protection the seal was wrapped in cloth or enclosed in a wooden box. From the seventeenth century a silver seal box was occasionally used, engraved or applied on the exterior with the arms on the seal. They were circular or otherwise shaped according to their contents. The boxes, which are sometimes called skippets, are occasionally found to have been given other uses; such as for holding snuff or cigarettes, or as inkstands.

SHAVING BASIN

A basin or dish with a deep centre and a broad flat rim with a semi-circular space to accommodate the neck of the person receiving the barber's attention is known in pottery and porcelain. Silver examples, mostly dating to pre-1750, are recorded, some of them accompanied by a hot-water jug and a soap box. They are invariably plain, matching only in their marks and mouldings and, if present, their armorials. Compact sets of shaving requisites have been noted as existing from most periods after the aforementioned date.

SHOE HORN

Queen Elizabeth I possessed a silver-gilt 'Shewinghorne' weighing 3 oz 5 dwt, but no further details of it are known. No doubt there were others, then and later, but they seem to have escaped being recorded.

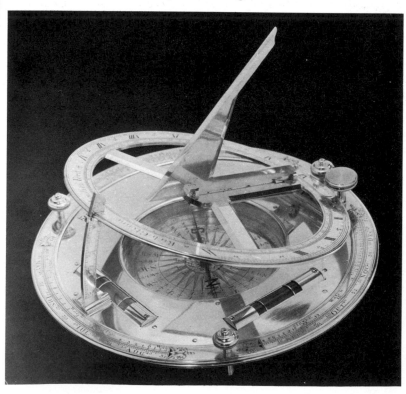

Microscope and accessories by Robert Rew, 1754. *Museum of the History of Science, Oxford.* The instrument is engraved 'Fra. Watkins Charing Cross London'; Watkins was a well-known supplier of optical and mathematical apparatus

Left
Universal Equinoctal Dial inscribed 'Rich: Glynne Londini Fecit', *c.* 1710. Diameter 17 cm. *The Time Museum, Rockford, Illinois*

SKEWER

Skewers for assisting in the carving of a joint were made in quantity in the years 1790–1830; earlier examples are recorded, but are scarce. The later ones are of flattened diamond section tapering to a point and with a ring or other terminal. Many were engraved with the crest of the owner to match spoons and forks and other tablewares. Meat skewers measure about 35 cm in length. Smaller versions, *c.* 15 cm long were for game, and all are more likely to be found nowadays serving as efficient paper-knives.

SKILLET

A skillet differs from a saucepan because it is raised on short legs, usually three in number, and frequently has a lid. Extant silver examples date from the seventeenth century and are few in number. One of 1685 has a curved spout like that found on some caudle cups.

SKIPPET *See* Seal box

SNUFF BOX

The taking of snuff became fashionable from the seventeenth century, and it was customary for a supply of the powder to be carried on the person. Small boxes were made for the purpose, many of them of silver and variously ornamented. In the early years of the nineteenth century their production centred in Birmingham. The boxes were stamped and cast in a great variety of patterns: views of public buildings and private mansions vying in popularity with figures of Harlequins, pedlars and hunting scenes. Some of the boxes were constructed with two or more compartments for different kinds of snuff, while others of larger size were made for the table rather than the pocket.

SNUFF MULL

In Scotland a snuff-container was termed a mull, its contents sneesh and the taking of it sneeshing. From *c.* 1680 the mull was vase-shaped, often constructed in the manner of a barrel from staves of various woods or ivory bound with hoops of silver. Some seventy

Snuffers and stand, maker's mark W B with a mullet below, *c.* 1685. Height 17.8 cm. *Sotheby's*

years later the favoured container was made from the end of a ram's horn, the pointed end curled so that it was no hazard, mounted in silver and the lid inset with a polished stone. Burns possessed one of this kind, inscribed on the silver lid 'ROBT. BURNS OFFICER OF THE EXCISE'. Large mulls were sometimes used at the dining table, and took the form of a ram's head complete with horns, the snuff container being mounted between the latter and topped by a cairngorm. Attached to it were a set of implements on chains; which might include a small hammer for dislodging any of the powder adhering to the side of the mull, a spike with which to break up lumps, a rake to smooth the surface, a spoon for taking snuff from the mull to the hand, and a hare's or rabbit's foot to make all neat and tidy. Many of these table mulls were fitted with wheels to ease their progress from diner to diner. Snuff-taking became less fashionable as the nineteenth century advanced, and by *c.* 1850 was rapidly losing its general appeal.

SNUFFERS and STAND

Until *c.* 1830, when a plaited self-consuming wick for candles was introduced, a wick curled over to cause what was termed guttering. It made the wax run to waste down the side of the candle, giving rise to black smoke and a noticeable loss of light. Guttering was prevented by trimming the wick, in some cases each half-hour, using a pair of snuffers: a scissors-action device that cut off the offending curl of wick. When not in use the snuffers rested in an upright stand or in a flat tray shaped more or less to the snuffers. The earliest recorded pairs of snuffers date from *c.* 1512 (British Museum) and *c.* 1550 (Victoria and Albert Museum). Pairs of seventeenth century date and later were made with both stands and trays, varying in ornament according to the style prevailing when they were made.

SOAP BOX

Soap in the form of a spherical ball could be kept in a silver-lidded container of similar shape raised on a low pedestal foot. The boxes date from the first half of the eighteenth century, and were either part of a shaving set of jug and basin or were a component of a toilet service. In the latter instance the soap box was usually accompanied by a matching box for holding a sponge, this last differing from the other by reason of having a pierced lid.

SOUP TUREEN

The covered soup tureen first appeared *c.* 1725 when it was of oval shape raised on a pedestal foot. It did not always, like later examples, have handles other than one on the cover. The oval form endured with occasional circular, rectangular and boat-shaped variants, with supports ranging from short feet to pedestals, and in due course including a matching stand. A few showed marked originality of design; in some cases the lid being decorated with a representation of the ingredients composing the contents or, less appropriately, in an essay in wild rococo, modelled as seated goats beneath a pile of fruit.

Soup tureens
(*left*) by Paul Crespin, 1740. Length 55.3 cm. *Toledo Museum, Ohio: photograph, Christie's.* It has been suggested that this outstandingly extravagant example of the rococo was the work of Crespin's neighbour and fellow-immigrant, Nicholas Sprimont

(*right*) by Paul de Lamerie, 1741. Length 45.1 cm. *Sotheby's*

(*left*) by Thomas Heming, 1771. Length 36 cm. *Phillips.* The engraved arms are those of George III

SOVEREIGN CASES for ATTACHING TO THE WATCH CHAIN.

To hold 5 sovereigns.

Silver, plain	...5/9, 7/6	9/0
„	Chased		10/0
„	Engine turned		10/0
„	Twist		15/0
Gold,	9 carat, plain		29/0
„	15 „ „		62/6
Metal, plated			1/8
„	Gilt		1/8

No. 192. Silver, combined sovereign purse and match box 16/3

Double Case, to hold 5 sovereigns and 6 half-sovereigns—

Silver, plain	....	19/0
Silver, chased	....	22/0
Gold, 9 carat, plain	....	69/0

Combined Sovereign and Postage Stamp Case.

Plain silver .... each 10/0

Sovereign cases shown in the catalogue of the Army & Navy Stores, London, 1898

SOVEREIGN CASE

Containers for gold sovereigns, which were gripped in spring-loaded spaces and could be slid out as required, were made in the nineteenth century. The Army and Navy Stores catalogue for 1898 listed several types, each with a ring for its attachment to a watch chain:

'Circular, and holding five sovereigns

Oval, to hold sovereigns and vesta matches

Rectangular, for sovereigns and postage stamps

Oval, holding five sovereigns and six half-sovereigns.'

All were silver, ranging in price from 5s 9d to 22s according to their complexity.

SOY FRAME

This was a silver frame fitted with a half-dozen or so small stoppered bottles holding sauces such as Soy: the latter prepared from the soy bean and originating in the Far East. Silver labels, small versions of wine labels, were suspended on the bottles to denote their contents, which included such brain-teasing and appetite-inducing flavourings as Cavich, Coratch and Piquante. The frames and labels date from *c.* 1800.

SPICE BOX

The earliest silver spice boxes are of shaped outline with the lid in the form of a realistic representation of a scallop shell. One of them, in the Ashmolean Museum, Oxford, has an actual shell inset in the top, and it has been suggested that this was the prototype. After *c.* 1660 an oval lidded casket, often referred to as a sugar box, may have been used for spice and have supplanted the first-mentioned type. Later, there was a limited demand for double-lidded boxes closely resembling French silver and ceramic *boîtes aux épices*.

SPONGE BOX *See* Soap box

SPOON

The earliest surviving spoons are attributed to the twelfth century. Understandably they are few in number, and it is uncertain whether they were made for use at the table or for a ceremonial purpose. At most times in the past the spoon, doubtless because of its obvious connection with food and the basis of life, has been more than just a table accessory. It was a present at a child's christening, but no less acceptable to a monarch from a subject as a New Year's gift. It was valued for its metal as well as for its function: a sixteenth-century writer warning his readers to safeguard their spoons when they were not in use – in the words of Charles Oman, 'a curious comment on the morals of diners or servants'.

By the fifteenth century a number of distinctive patterns of spoons had been introduced and retained their popularity until the Restoration. From being circular or a pointed oval the bowl became what is termed fig-shaped: oval, but narrower where it joins the stem or stalk. Most attention, however, was paid to the top of the stem, the knop, which varied considerably in design. The types of knops, which were often gilt, included the undermentioned.

Acorn With the rough-surfaced cup joined to the stem and the fruit uppermost, sometimes with leaves. The earliest is *c.* 1300.

Baluster In the shape of a series of mouldings resembling a staircase banister: the latter word being a corruption of baluster. Examples are usually of sixteenth/ seventeenth-century date.

Diamond Point Has a pointed top with facets like a cut stone. The design dates back to at least the fifteenth century.

Lion Sejant Shows the King's Beast in seated pose, facing either forward or to one side. Most examples are datable to the sixteenth or seventeenth century.

Spoons (*right*)
(*a*) Maidenhead, 1595. *Sotheby's*
(*b*) Seal top, *c.* 1617. *Sotheby, King and Chasemore*
(*c*) Slip top, *c.* 1650. *Royal Albert Memorial Museum, Exeter*
(*d*) Wrythen, *c.* 1580. *Royal Albert Memorial Museum, Exeter*
(*e*) 'The Master', 1586. *Phillips*
(*f*) Elizabethan Worthies, 'The Tichborne Spoons', by Christopher Wace, 1592. Silver-gilt. *Christie's*

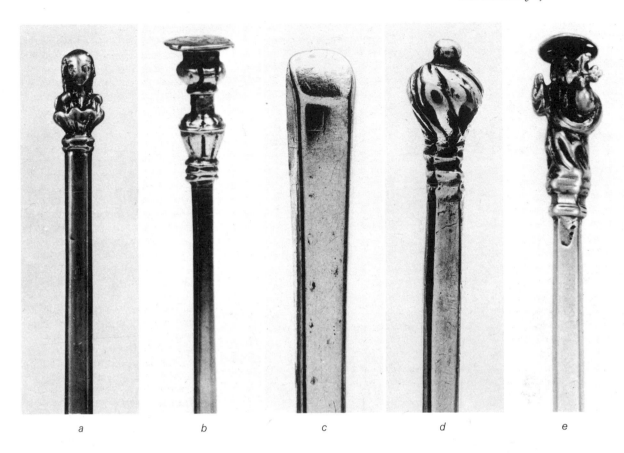

a   b   c   d   e

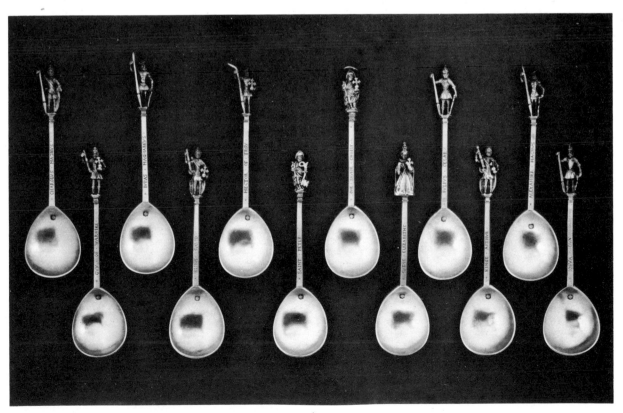

f

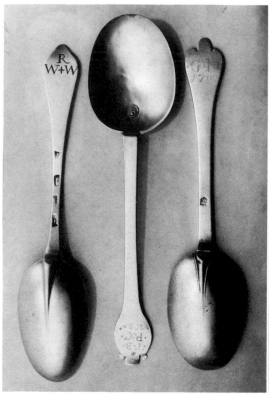
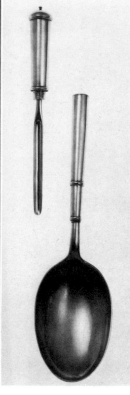

(*above*) Dognose and two Trefids,
c. 1700. Length *c.* 15 cm.
(*right*) Basting spoon by John Barrett,
1751. Length 35 cm. *Phillips.* The handle
conceals a detachable marrow scoop

Maidenhead With the bust of a
   woman, sometimes said to
   represent the Virgin Mary.
   Current from *c.* 1500–1600.
Moor's Head So called, but possibly
   intended as the head of Christ as
   a child. Specimens date to the
   sixteenth century and are rare.
Puritan Not really a knop but a
   termination; the rectangular
   stem, broadening at the top, is cut
   at a right angle and sometimes is
   notched. It acquired its name
   from its plain appearance and
   because of its popularity *c.* 1650.
Seal Top Has a short series of
   mouldings surmounted by a
   circular or hexagonal flat-topped
   disc that is often found pricked,
   scratched or engraved with
   initials and/or a date. Current
   c. 1550 for about a century.
Slip Top Having the top of the stem
   neatly cut at an angle. A
   specimen of 1487 is recorded, and
   a will of 1498 mentions spoons
   'slipped in lez stalkes'. They

continued to be made until
shortly after 1650.
Wodewose The 'green Man' or wild
   man of the woods, famed in early
   legends, is depicted with his
   club. An example of 1460 is in the
   Victoria and Albert Museum and
   a few others are known.
Wrythen Has a knop in the form of a
   spherical or egg-shaped knob
   with spiral fluting. Examples date
   from the fifteenth and sixteenth
   centuries.
In addition to the foregoing were
spoons having their stems
surmounted by figures of the
twelve Apostles, each carrying his
attribute in the right hand,
completed by the figure of the
Master, each of the thirteen
wearing a halo or nimbus.
Complete sets are of extreme rarity,
the earliest being dated 1527.
Known examples of part-sets and
single specimens date from *c.* 1460.
   A single recorded set of twelve
spoons is ornamented with figures
of biblical, classical and romantic
heroes, the so-called Worthies who
were highly esteemed in the
sixteenth century.
   After the Restoration the
long-enduring types were

superseded by a variety of designs
introduced during the course of the
succeeding century. The first of
them was the Trefid, developed
from the notched Puritan which
was given a flat stem broadened at
the top and with two V-shaped
cuts. Beneath the bowl the stem
was extended to a long point, the
'rat-rail', and the bowl itself became
oval in outline. This pattern duly
became the 'Old English', with the
stem thickened at the top and
slightly curled. Other designs that
achieved acceptance included the
Fiddle, with the stem resembling in
shape a violin; Threaded Fiddle,
like the preceding but bordered by
a narrow thread-like raised border;
and King's Pattern, topped by a
shell above two anthemions
(honeysuckle flowers) placed end
to end. Some tea and other spoons
were attractively stamped with
raised designs *c.* 1750–1800; rare
examples bear political inscriptions
such as 'I love Liberty', others have
Masonic signs or the Prince of
Wales's feathers.
   In addition to spoons with which
to eat or for ceremonial use, there
were others for special purposes.
Among them the following:
Basting or Hash Spoon With long
   handles and large-sized oval
   bowls.
Mote Skimmer or *Strainer Spoon*: of
   teaspoon size with a pierced bowl
   and pointed knop, intended for
   removing unwanted tealeaves
   from a cup and for unblocking
   the spout of a teapot. They were
   occasionally used for straining
   wine and there are records of
   them for that use in church plate.
   See Caddy spoon.

SPOON TRAY
Small trays to hold teaspoons were
in use during the first half-dozen
decades of the eighteenth century.
They varied in size, shape and
decoration and were made with
and without feet.

SPURS
Silver spurs for horse-riding
survive from the eighteenth
century. They usually have steel
rowels held in decorative silver
fittings, with leather straps for
attaching them to the rider's boots.
Spurs were worn also by fighting

cocks, the curved and sharply-pointed silver spikes being similarly mounted in leather. At Colonial Williamsburg is a set of six cockspurs of *c.* 1770 in their original shagreen-covered case. It bears the engraved trade card of Samuel Toulmin 'at the Dial and Crown near Hungerford Market in the Strand'.

STIRRUP CUP
The stirrup cup was made to contain a stimulating and convivial drink taken in the saddle before moving off. Current from *c.* 1760 until the early decades of the nineteenth century, it was modelled in silver in a variety of appropriate forms, the most common being a fox's mask. Other open-air sports were similarly

Sugar box, maker's mark I intersecting S, 1676. Length 19 cm. *Bonhams*

Stirrup cup in the form of a hare's mask by Rebecca Emes and Edward Barnard, 1809. The interior gilt, height 17.8 cm. *Sotheby's*

served by means of cups in the shape of greyhounds' and hares' masks. Among recorded rarities is a set of four cups, hall-marked 1802, made in the form of stag hoofs.

STRAINER
Strainers dating from the eighteenth century are often referred to as orange strainers, although there can be little doubt that their use was not limited to any

one fruit. A few pre-1700 examples are known, each with one or two handles that are either tubular or flat and pierced. Their design becomes more elaborate as the years pass, with beautifully patterned piercing in the bowl and handles of complex design. For tea there was the mote skimmer or strainer spoon, that was eventually succeeded by a small-sized strainer of similar pattern to those described above. *See* Spoon (Mote skimmer or strainer).

STRAWBERRY DISH
Silver dishes with distinctive fluted upcurving sides are often referred to as having been used for serving

strawberries. They range in diameter from *c.* 12–25 cm, and can equally well have been used for any other food.

SUGAR BASIN, BASKET, BOWL and BOX
An oval casket or box with a hinged cover surmounted by an entwined handle is generally termed a sugar box. Examples date from *c.* 1660 and were perhaps an alternative to the cylindrical caster that came into use at that time. It is possible that the box held lumps of sugar broken from a sugar-loaf, while a caster was for the same substance reduced

Sweetmeat basket, and companion perhaps for cream, by Henry Chawner, 1790. Lengths 15 and 12.5 cm. *Sotheby Bearne*

Tankards (*right*)
(*a*) by William Ramsay, Newcastle, *c.* 1690. Height 21.1 cm. *Sotheby, King and Chasemore*
(*b*) by William Ged, Edinburgh, 1715. Height 20.3 cm. *Sotheby's*
(*c*) by Thomas Heming, 1746. Height 19 cm. *King and Chasemore*
(*d*) maker's mark T S in monogram crowned, 1683. Height 17.8 cm. *Sotheby's*

to powder in a mortar. The box fell out of use soon after 1700, but re-appeared differently shaped *en suite* with a pair of tea caddies *c.* 1730. The sugar bowl with a detachable cover was first made at the close of the seventeenth century, an example of 1691 having a turned finial. By *c.* 1715 such a finial had been replaced by a shallow raised rim that enabled the lid to be stood upside-down in the manner of a paten; a type of bowl and cover much copied in Chinese porcelain exported to the West. Many of the bowls lost their covers over the years and in their lidless form were the prototypes of sugar basins, which were open-topped and often had two handles. In the second half of the eighteenth century the bowl was raised on a tall foot and was given a hinged handle, so becoming a circular or boat-shaped sugar basket. Those in neo-classical taste were pierced and engraved and given blue glass liners. Early in the next century, when gilt table services were the fashion, some of them included pairs or sets of covered vase-shaped sugar containers and stands comparable to those that were then part of a china dessert service.

SUGAR NIPPERS and TONGS
Sugar servers were at first similar in pattern to fire tongs, having a pivoted hinge or an arrangement of springy arcs with oval grips to hold the sugar. From *c.* 1720–60 they were replaced by nippers of scissors-like construction with grips in the shape of shells; a type that is only occasionally fully hall-marked. The enduring one-piece tongs appeared *c.* 1780.

SWEETMEAT BASKET
Small baskets or bowls, with and without hinged handles, were used for holding sweetmeats. They were to be found suspended from the arms of an epergne, but were probably also sold singly or in sets.

SWORD HILT *See* Military plate

TABLE SERVICE
A service of knives, forks and spoons, all alike as regards pattern and marks is termed a table service, but if details vary then strictly it should be named a 'matched' service. The latter are not uncommon, for as services passed from generation they were often divided among legatees or were added to, and it was not unusual for a service to be matched up by a retailer when he first sold it. He might not have had sufficient stock to fill an order, and would buy what he lacked from fellow-tradesmen. It is impossible to be precise about the quantity of each item that should be present in a service: its composition varied according to the purse of the buyer and his household requirements. The items would include knives, forks and spoons in table and dessert sizes, and after *c.* 1750 dessert knives and forks and a variety of spoons and ladles for salt, mustard, and so forth, all of them in dozens except for the last group. After *c.* 1800 the list could be extended to include ice spoons, grape scissors and much else.

TANKARD
The earliest surviving tankards date from the mid-sixteenth century and are pear-shaped on a low foot with a hinged cushion lid. These were followed by vessels of tapering cylindrical form, resembling the taller flagons of the period. During the seventeenth century tankards became shorter and wider, retaining their cylindrical outline, and the lids varied from flat to slightly domed. In the next century they reverted to domed lids, and *c.* 1730 were given curved bases on short moulded feet: the so-called tucked in base seen also on coffee pots and other vessels. By 1790 the tankard was less often in use, drinking from a glass being preferred.

TAPER BOX
The cylindrical box, resembling a mustard pot but with a hole in the lid and lacking a handle, was made to contain a coil of wax taper. This was led through the hole, lighted, and used to melt sealing-wax in the days before gummed envelopes were available. The box dates from *c.* 1700 and is sometimes termed a bougie box; *bougie* being French for a wax candle.

TAZZA
A low-sided bowl or dish on a tall foot, sometimes with a cover, was known as a *tazza*, apparently adopted from the Arabic *tassah*, a basin. The article was often decorated with chasing, and some examples are to be found among church plate. The tazza was a sixteenth-century form that re-emerged a century later as the footed salver, differing in that the rim of the latter was only slightly raised and the foot was less tall.

TEA CADDY
A container holding a small quantity of tea came into use during the last decades of the seventeenth century, when it was known as a canister. Later the word caddy was applied to it, the word being adapted from the Malay *kati*: a kati being the weight of *c.* 540 g (about 1⅓ lb) by which the leaf was sold in the East. The early canisters or caddies were mostly of rectangular section with a short round neck closed by a cap cover. This last served as a measure when dispensing the contents, and to facilitate filling the top or base of the article was constructed to slide out. Caddies were usually made in pairs, one being for Green tea (*Thea viridis*) and the other for Bohea (*Thea Bohea*). A third container, of conforming pattern, was sometimes provided for sugar, and by 1740 there were sets of the three available in neat boxes of wood, inlaid or veneered with mother-of-pearl and other exotic materials. They were invariably provided with locks and keys and sometimes fitted with silver corner-mounts, handles and escutcheons. Other shapes of caddies were produced from time to time, and there were examples in

a

b

c

e

d

f

Tea caddies

(*a*) by Paul de Lamerie, 1724. Height 13.3 cm. *Christie's*

(*b*) by John Parker and Edward Wakelin, 1763. Height 10.8 cm. *Sothebys*

(*c*) by Robert Hennell, 1788. Height 12.7 cm. *Sotheby, King and Chasemore*

(*d*) by Edward Vincent, 1774. Height 11.5 cm. *Phillips*. This is shown with its original leather-covered protective case.

(*e*) by Paul de Lamerie, 1744. Height c. 13 cm. *Christie's*

(*f*) by Rebecca Emes and Edward Barnard, 1809. *King and Chasemore*. This example has two compartments for different teas, each with a lockable hinged lid

Toilet service by Daniel Garnier, 1696.
Height of mirror-frame 61 cm. *Christie's.*
See page 143

Wine cooler by Philip Rollos, *c.* 1715–20.
Height 29.6 cm. Ickworth, Suffolk: *The
National Trust: photo, Bridgeman Art
Library.* One of a pair, each bearing the
coat of arms of the first Earl of Bristol.
See page 146

Set of three caddies, cream jug, sugar nips, two knives, a mote skimmer or straining spoon, and twelve tea spoons, all by Paul de Lamerie, 1735; the complete equipage contained in a mahogany case 29 cm in length. *Leeds City Art Galleries*

the form of small vases as well as others of boat shape with a pedestal foot. With the coming of cheaper tea, largely because of imports from India, the caddy fell out of use. In the 1850s it was noted by Henry Mayhew that dealers in secondhand goods disposed of the outdated wooden boxes to working people, who found them useful for holding pawn tickets.

TEA KETTLE

When taking tea it was necessary to have at hand a source of boiling water, and the tea kettle with its stand and heater filled that role. The article was first made in the 1680s, John Hervey buying one in 1697 when he noted: 'Paid Mr. Chambers his bill in full for a Tea-kettle & lampe, weight 90 ounces 11 dwt. at 6s. 2d.', a sum of *c.* £30. The earlier examples have the stand separate and with handles for carrying it, but before long the stand was affixed to the base of the kettle by two removable pins on chains. The pin at the back could be removed, leaving the other to serve as a hinge to allow the kettle to tilt for pouring. Because of its size the kettle was the subject of ornament stressing its importance. Engraving and chasing were employed as fashion demanded, and the sides were frequently utilised for the owner's coat of arms. At first the stand rested on four feet, but later

examples were given three, and in some cases the whole stood on a matching round or triangular tray. There have survived a few exceptional kettles complete with tall silver stands, the latter with tripod bases, knopped stems and, in some examples, a dished top similar to the wooden tables on which the majority of kettles must have stood. The kettle was largely supplanted when the tea-urn was introduced in the 1760s, but it continued to be made in small numbers for several more decades. In the nineteenth century the kettle and stand was revived in the form of near-copies of those popular in earlier days.

TEAPOT

It was in 1615 that an agent of the East India Company arriving in Japan wrote to a colleague in Macao

Teapot, maker's mark T L, 1670. Height 34.3 cm. *Victoria and Albert Museum.* An inscription on the pot records that it was presented to the Committee of the East India Company in 1670.

requesting 'a pot of the best sort of *chaw*'. Later in the century, in 1658, the 'China Drink called by the Chineans *Tcha*, by other nations *Tay*, alias *Tee*' was to be tasted in London, and shortly afterwards the leaf was offered for sale. On 25 September 1660 Samuel Pepys took his first cup of the new beverage, but did not record his opinion of the experience. It was not long before it was accepted nationally, and a range of articles for its preparation and imbibing had to be devised. It was predictable that the country whence came the tea should provide the inspiration, and two surviving silver-gilt examples of *c.* 1690 are copies of Chinese wine pots. Charles Oman has drawn attention to the fact that unlike many other silver articles, silver teapots are deservedly esteemed more for their beauty than for their rarity. This applies not least to those dating from early in the eighteenth century, which were in two principal patterns: pear-shaped and sometimes also faceted, or spherical and known as 'bullet' teapots. Variations of these shapes, with and without chasing, persisted until *c.* 1770, when there was a liking for pots of oval section. After *c.* 1810 preference was for a round-cornered rectangle, or cushion, which later appeared as a round cushion. Shapes changed constantly during the nineteenth century, but no more often than did the popularity of successive styles of chased, cast and engraved ornament.

Teapots (*right*)
(*a*) by Pentecost Symons, Exeter, 1712. Height 21 cm. *Bearnes, Torquay.* Symons worked at Plymouth, Exeter being his nearest office for assaying and marking
(*b*) bullet shaped by Francis Nelme, 1724. Height *c.* 11 cm. *King and Chasemore*
(*c*) by Richard Watts, 1712. Height 14 cm. *Sotheby's*
(*d*) by Hester Bateman, 1785. Height 12.7 cm. *Sotheby's. See also* Tea Services

TEA SERVICE

Tea services comprising matching
components appeared at the close
of Queen Anne's reign. One of
three pieces and another of five
pieces, both hall-marked 1713, are
recorded, and they continued to be
produced spasmodically during the
century. Sometimes the various
items match in appearance but
differ in date and maker suggesting
they were purchased piecemeal or
were assembled by a retailer. After
1800 services appeared regularly
and in quantity, often complete
with tea kettle, coffee pot and tray.

Tea services
Tea service by John Scofield, 1790.
Christie's

(*above*) Tea service by Paul Storr, 1822.
Phillips
(*below*) Tea service by Walker and Hall,
Sheffield, 1885/95. *Sotheby, King and
Chasemore*. This service includes a
coffee pot

(*above*) Tea service by Henry Wilkinson and Co., Sheffield, 1833. *King and Chasemore*
(*below*) Tea service by E. and J. Barnard, 1860. *Sotheby, King and Chasemore*

Tea urn by Peter and William Bateman, 1806. Height *c*. 45 cm. *Bonhams*

TEA URN
The tea urn provided boiling water at the tea table, replacing the kettle from *c*. 1760 and remaining popular for about fifty years. It was fitted with a tap at a convenient height above the base, so did not require tilting like a kettle. The urn was ideally suited to neo-classical taste, and its gracefully-shaped body was often fluted to conform.
Small-sized, square-topped tables of *c*. 1760 onwards, with a pull-out flap at the front, are known as urn tables and were used to support the urn.

THIMBLE
Silver thimbles were made in the days of Elizabeth I, but there are few remaining that are datable to before 1700. Over the years their shape varied from tall to squat, but being functional objects of small size the scope for decorative treatment was usually limited to a band of ornament round the base. Few thimbles bear marks because their light weight excused them from assay and hall-marking, so they can be dated only by the style of any decoration present.

TOASTED CHEESE DISH
The dish was usually oblong in shape, sometimes with a compartment for hot water in the base above which were a number of small shallow dishes. The hinged lid was detachable in some cases, and the wooden handle was placed at the back below the hinge. The dishes held pieces of toast on each of which was a slice of cheese, and when placed in front of a fire the open lid reflected heat on to the food while protecting the hand of anyone gripping the handle. The dishes were made during the years 1770–1820.

TOASTING FORK
Silver toasting forks are known to have existed in the mid-sixteenth century and one engraved with the date 1561, but not hall-marked, survives in confirmation. It has two prongs like those of a carving fork, and between them a third bent back to point towards the handle. Others of various patterns and dates are known, most of them having wooden handles *c*. 1 m in length. John Hervey owned one, recording in his diary in 1711: 'July 26. Paid Mr. Chambers for mending ye silver toaster, £1. 2. 0.' [£1.10].

TOAST RACK
Silver toast racks were made from *c*. 1770. There were three types: with an open base, with a solid base, and made to fold in the manner of a trellis. Most of them were plainly constructed of wire, but a proportion, including some made by Paul Storr, were of elaborate design.

TOBACCO BOX
Old tobacco boxes of pocketable size made of silver and of other materials with silver mounts, exist in large numbers. Many were used to carry tobacco, in the leaf or as snuff, but there can be little doubt that just as many held other substances. William Hone in his *Year Book* described at length the tobacco box belonging to the overseers of the poor at Westminster. He tells that the pocket-size box was of silver-mounted horn and had been bought by a parishioner for 4d in 1713. It had been given at the time to a society of former overseers, successive chairmen adding more silver to the original gift. By 1832, when Hone wrote, it had become encased in four outer boxes 'until the whole has become of greater bulk and worth than any tobacco-box in the kingdom'.

TOILET SERVICE

The toilet service displayed on a dressing table became a striking and fashionable feature of a lady's bedroom at the time of the Restoration. In 1673 Sir Thomas Myddelton, of Chirk Castle, noted in his accounts under the date 27 September:

'ffor Plate &c. given by him [Sir Thomas] to his sist^r m^{ris} Mary Myddelton upon her marryadge to m^r St J^{no} Bennet, viz: for 1 combe box, 2 powder boxes, 2 patch boxes & 2 brushes weighing 66 oz., at 5^s 10^d p oz.   £19. 5.0.

ffor Graueing ye plate with mantle, coate & Crest   0.18.0.

For searching out the coate of Armes   0. 1.0.

Toilet service, *c.* 1680. Height of looking-glass frame, 66 cm. *Sotheby's*

Several services survive from about that date, all of them varying in their components, although it is likely that some have become separated over the years. Many included a framed looking-glass to match the other items, which could include scent bottles, a box with pincushion top, and candlesticks in addition to those already mentioned. The comb box bought by Sir Thomas Myddelton would have been of a size to hold the combs of the time; which were double-sided, with coarse teeth along one length and fine along the other, measuring overall *c.* 15 by 10 cm. The services followed designs current at the time they were made, their manufacture virtually ceasing at the close of the eighteenth century. They were supplanted by portable ones in fitted travelling boxes, these in turn being superseded by services of silver-mounted cut-glass in leather cases. Portable services were made also for men, their contents including such male requisites as razors and shaving brush, scissors, boot hooks, penknife and screwdriver, as well as silver-lidded bottles.

TRAVELLING CANTEEN

Mealtime accessories for use when travelling were made in silver from the late seventeenth century onwards. The principal component was a drinking-cup into which fitted a variety of other items that included a knife, fork and spoon, spice-box, corkscrew and a nutmeg grater, but the contents were not standardised and varied according to requirements. While some canteens were provided for use when on the road, others were carried when campaigning.

Travelling lamp by William F. Wright, 1898. *Sotheby, King and Chasemore.* The two views show the lamp open and closed

Below
Pair of tumblers by Anthony Nelme, 1710. Height 7 cm. *Sotheby, King and Chasemore.* On the left-hand one is seen the scratch weight: 7 oz 15 dwt

TRAVELLING LAMP

Travellers were catered for by the provision of folding portable reading-lamps, some of which were of silver. Each held a candle in a spring-loaded tube, so that the source of light was in the same position irrespective of the length of the candle. At the rear of the case was a sharp hook by which it could be fixed in the upholstery at the back of a seat in a coach or railway-carriage.

TRAY

The tray originated in the salver, of which it gradually became an enlarged version with the addition of a pair of handles. These were incorporated either in the decorative flat border, or where an upright pierced one was present the handles were cut into it at opposite sides. The size of the tray was dictated by the growth in number and capacity of the items in the tea equipage.

TUMBLER

Tumblers were drinking-cups with rounded bases, so that if knocked and tipped they would return to an upright position. Samuel Pepys bought two in October 1664, but there are a few earlier mentions of their existence. Sometimes they were made in sets that fitted one in another, and at Colonial Williamsburg is a nest of half-a-dozen tumblers of *c.* 1680 complete with a lid. Like many others they are matt on the exterior, which is a decorative way of providing a sure grip.

VASE

Shortly after the Restoration a set of large silver vases was an accepted way of displaying one's wealth and position. The vases were made in pairs and in sets of three or more, in

Right
Vase, 'The Tennyson Vase', by C. F. Hancock, 1867. Parcel-gilt. Height *c.* 80 cm. *Christie's.* It was designed by Henry Hugh Armstead R.A. and depicts scenes from the 'Idylls of the King'; the vase was displayed by Hancocks at the Paris Exhibition of 1867 and in 1887 was awarded to the winner of the Royal Jubilee Cup at Ascot

the manner of Continental pottery prototypes that were copied in Oriental porcelain. The silver versions were elaborately chased and stood an average of 50 cm in height. The fashion for them was revived *c.* 1860, when copies of the earlier ones were made. In the eighteenth century, two-handled vases or covered cups were in favour, de Lamerie and others producing outstanding examples. Later came others of neo-classical design that were especially popular as prizes at horse races. From early in the nineteenth century a popular subject was the Warwick Vase, this serving as a winecooler as well as being a decorative object. *See* Cup, Lloyd's patriotic fund vase, Warwick vase.

VINAIGRETTE
The vinaigrette is a small container with a hinged lid, the opening of which reveals a hinged and pierced inner cover. Beneath the latter was a piece of sponge soaked in a strong-smelling mixture of vinegar (acetic acid) with camphor and other pungent substances. Silver examples, with gilt interiors to prevent corrosion, were made in large numbers from *c.* 1775 for a period of about 100 years. The majority came from Birmingham, where the silversmiths specialised in making small boxes and novelties. The contents of the vinaigrette were inhaled when occasion demanded, its purposes being to ward off evil spirits in the form of germs, unpleasant smells, and incipient faintness.

WAITER *See* Salver and waiter

WARMING PAN
The circular metal pan with a pierced lid and long handle was filled with charcoal and used to warm a bed, and it may be wondered that it did not cause numerous conflagrations. Most of the pans were of copper or brass, but sometimes silver was employed. Pepys was given one of the latter on New Year's Day 1669 by Captain Beckford, a supplier of clothing to the Navy. The diarist

noted that he was doubtful whether it was correct for him to accept it, but did not record if he overcame his scruples.

WARWICK VASE

The antique marble Warwick Vase was discovered at Rome in the grounds of Hadrian's Villa when a pool was drained in 1770. It was bought by Sir William Hamilton, British Ambassador at Naples and a well-known antiquarian. He, in turn, sold it to his nephew the Earl of Warwick, who placed it in a specially constructed building at Warwick Castle. Reduced copies of the Vase were made in pottery, bronze and silver, followed by full-size reproductions in bronze and an unsuccessful attempt to do the same in silver. The small silver versions were popular from *c.* 1812 and throughout the century. The original remained at Warwick Castle for 200 years, when it was sold and is now owned by Glasgow Art Galleries and Museum.

WAX JACK

The wax jack held a coil of waxed taper, vertically or horizontally, led through a spring-loaded grip that held it steady when lighted. It was a variant of the taper box and the taper stick, likewise used for melting sealing-wax. The wax jack came into use soon after the Restoration and continued to be made for the ensuing 100 years.

Warwick Vase by Barnard and Co., 1901. Diameter 33 cm. *Sotheby, King and Chasemore*

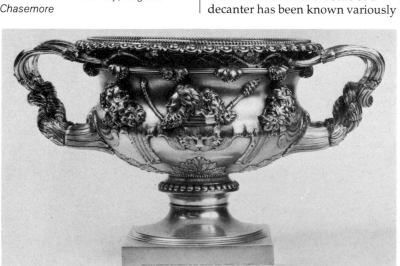

WINE BOTTLE

Imposing silver vessels to hold wine dating from the late sixteenth century form part of the significant collection of English plate in the Kremlin, Moscow. This was acquired as a result of visits paid to Russia by English embassies and Russian visits to England, both of which gave and received costly presents. Post-Restoration wine bottles are not plentiful, the most popular shape in which they were made being that of a pilgrim's flask. This has flattened sides, a tall neck and loose chain handles, an average height of *c.* 40 cm, and a weight rising to 90 oz.

WINE CISTERN

The wine cistern was a large vessel in which were placed bottles of wine to cool their contents. It was among the objects that came into use following the Restoration, when owners of them vied in owning larger and heavier examples. The largest extant cooler is 1.7 m wide, weighs 7221 oz and is now in the Hermitage Museum, Leningrad, having been made in London in 1734–5. Another of 1829 is almost as large and as heavy, and is now at Windsor Castle. On 31 August 1830, on the occasion of the birthday of William IV, the maker of the cistern, John Bridge, requested the privilege of being present 'and was hid during the dinner behind the great wine cooler'.

WINE COASTER

This stand for a wine-bottle or a decanter has been known variously

Wine bottle by John Bodington, 1699. Silver-gilt, height 42.5 cm. *Sotheby's.* One of a pair engraved with Royal arms

as a decanter stand, a bottle stand and a wine slide; all of which describe its purpose. Most examples were given wooden bases with baize beneath, so they could be slid from diner to diner without harming the polished surface of a table. Coasters began to be made in the 1760s, the majority of them with pierced sides of scrolling or other design incorporating a blank space for the engraving of a crest or initials. From *c.* 1820 more costly examples were made, designed with appropriate scenes of Bacchanalian children amid vines, gilt and with silver bases. All were supplied in pairs or in multiples of two but only occasionally exceeding a half-dozen. Twin coasters in the form of a jolly-boat were made *c.* 1800, and later came others mounted on wheels and with places for the decanter stoppers when they were removed.

WINE COOLER

The wine cooler or ice pail came into use *c.* 1700, changing little in basic form from then until *c.* 1830;

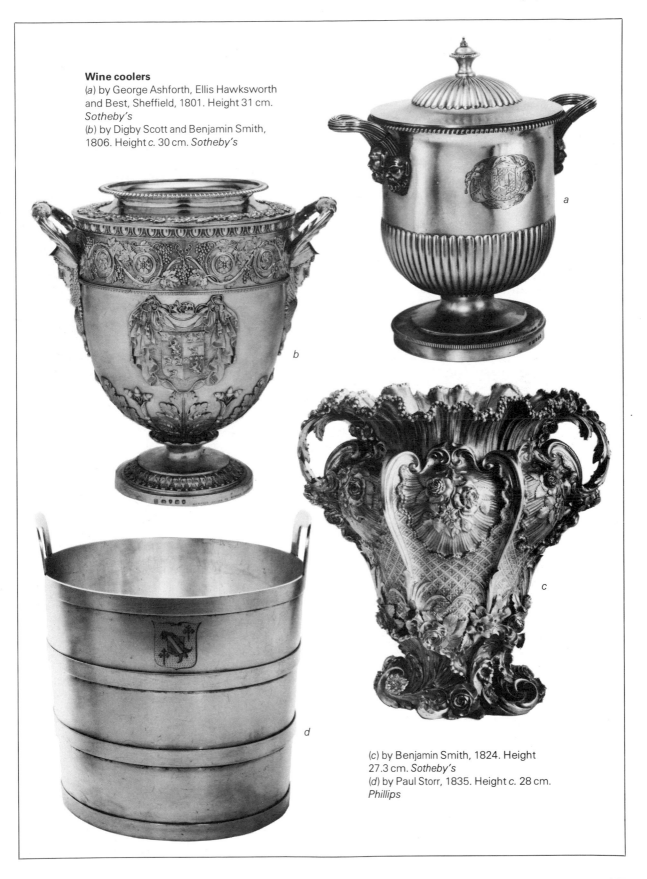

Wine coolers
(*a*) by George Ashforth, Ellis Hawksworth and Best, Sheffield, 1801. Height 31 cm. *Sotheby's*
(*b*) by Digby Scott and Benjamin Smith, 1806. Height *c.* 30 cm. *Sotheby's*

(*c*) by Benjamin Smith, 1824. Height 27.3 cm. *Sotheby's*
(*d*) by Paul Storr, 1835. Height *c.* 28 cm. *Phillips*

thenceforward seldom being made of silver, porcelain being preferred. The cooler held a single bottle, as opposed to the wine cistern that held several. The shape of the vessel was determined by its use, and in most instances decoration centred in an applied or engraved coat of arms. Many of the coolers were made with internal liners and removable rims, so that the ice and water was kept from direct contact with the bottle. Normally supplied in pairs, they are sometimes found in larger numbers in multiples of two.

WINE FOUNTAIN

A silver-gilt fountain was listed in 1574 and was complete with six pillars and a pipe surmounted appropriately by the figure of a woman holding a bunch of grapes. Surviving examples dating *c.* 1680–1730 are more aptly described as urns, being large vase-like vessels, some standing over 1 m in height, each complete with a tap at the base. Some of the fountains are *en suite* with wine cisterns.

WINE FUNNEL

Funnels for decanting wine appeared soon after the mid-seventeenth century, about the time when bottles began to bear the name, crest, arms, or initials of their owner stamped on a glass seal. The bottles would have been filled from a cask and a funnel for the purpose was a necessity. Early examples are scarce, but there are plenty dating from after *c.* 1770. Being functional articles, funnels were devoid of ornament, although the later ones generally had a gadrooned or otherwise decorated rim. These last were often fitted with a strainer and had a matching stand.

WINE LABEL

The wine label, known sometimes as a bottle ticket, dates from the mid-eighteenth century, and took the place of the 'label' engraved on a glass decanter. The silver version varied in shape and decoration over the years, and has received much attention in modern times: attention directed no less to its

appearance and history than to the lettering borne on it, whether engraved, cast or pierced. The names on the labels have created an interest in long-forgotten wines and other beverages; demonstrating how pleasing trifles can contain in themselves unsuspected aspects of social history. Similar remarks apply to the small-sized labels made for sauce bottles. They have been recorded with names ranging from

the still-familiar Soy to the exotic-sounding and unremembered Zoobditty-Match: probably a fish sauce of Indian origin. Sauce labels had short lengths of chain by which to hang them on the bottles. Most wine labels were equipped similarly, but there were a few alternatives: among them a plain or twisted wire ring, a combination of chain and wire, and the label itself in the form of a neck ring.

Wine labels
'Madeira' (*top*) by Charles Rawlings and William Summers, 1829
'Lemon' by Mary and Charles Reily, 1827
'Port' by John Riley, 1823
'Bronti' by John Yapp and John Woodward, Birmingham, 1846
'Madeira' (*centre*) by Hester Bateman, *c.* 1780

'Sherry' by Samuel Meriton, *c.* 1780
'Champagne' by Sandylands Drinkwater, *c.* 1750
'Hollands' by John Taylor and John Perry, Birmingham, 1836
'Teneriffe' and 'Madeira' (*bottom*) by Peter and William Bateman, 1812
'Mountain' *c.* 1810. All *Bonhams*

The Care of Silver

One of the beauties of silver is its rewarding response to care; the shine of a well-tended example indicating the energy expended on it. The surface of the metal is subject to tarnishing caused by the presence of sulphur in the atmosphere or in nearby paint, fabric and other materials. Sulphur combines with silver to form a film of silver sulphide that dims the shine and eventually blackens the article.

In the past, owners sometimes returned their pieces to a silversmith for refurbishing and overhaul; entries in accounts make mention of the practice. Thus, in 1727 the Earl of Bristol paid David Willaume approximately 50p 'for boyling and mending old plate', without specifying the items involved, and in 1738 Sir Robert Walpole paid George Wickes the equivalent of £1.50p 'for byling and doing up a turreen as new'. Across the Atlantic a similar method prevailed, again relying on water. Martha Gandy Fales reprinted an advertisement from the *South Carolina Gazette* of 30 December 1760 in which John-Paul Grimke of Charleston notified readers of the arrival of a consignment of goods from London. He concluded the announcement by informing his customers:

> '. . . as he has lost his boy in the small-pox, who used to go to their houses to clean their plate, he takes this method to acquaint them of an easy way, by which their own servants may clean the same, without spoiling the chased work, *viz.* Wash your plate in warm water with a little soap dissolved therein; Wipe it dry with a clean towel; then brush it with whiting dissolved in rum or any other spirits; which will restore to it its former beauty and brightness again. NB He has brushes enough to sell.'

It is to be hoped that Mr Grimke's brushes had reasonably soft bristles, so that the metal did not suffer scratches as a result of their use. The metal is subject to damage not only from pollution of the atmosphere, but from the careless use of harmful materials.

The twentieth-century owner of old silver has available several reliable ways of keeping his possessions in good condition. The paramount condition in employing any of them is to minimise abrasion. All cleaning of silver must involve the removal of some of the actual metal. In the past some articles were engraved under the base with their weight, the so-called scratch weight, and re-weighing today invariably reveals a lower figure. It has been stated that a couple of centuries of regular polishing results in the removal from an article of an amount between 5 and 15 dwt.

There are a number of ways of polishing that do their best to keep wear-and-tear to a minimum, while producing a satisfactory shine and preserving a fraction of our heritage for the enjoyment of future generations. It is a matter of personal choice which of them is employed. The various possibilities include the following, which are not listed in any particular order.

Warm or hot water and a little soap

As mentioned above, this was used in the past. It is excellent for articles that are in constant use and do not get noticeably tarnished. Soap means good old-fashioned soap, and not a substitute such as a detergent. On the whole it is preferable to avoid the use of a detergent for this purpose, however good it may be for so many others.

Electro-chemical process

The article to be cleaned is placed in contact with some aluminium, for example a piece of baking-foil, in a solution of warm water with a teaspoonful of ordinary washing soda (sodium carbonate) so that the object is immersed completely. When the tarnish has gone, remove the piece of silver and polish it with cotton-wool or a soft cloth.

Powder

Plate powders were formerly the butler's standby, and probably still are in the diminished number of homes with a butler on the staff. In 1839 Joseph Goddard devised a polish in powder form that was marketed under his name for over a century, and several generations of its buyers carefully mixed it with methylated spirits, as instructed, and then rubbed away the pink stuff where it had been applied. Goddard's Plate Powder had the drawback of requiring painstaking and thorough removal, or tell-tale traces remained in the crevices of chased and other ornament.

Dipping

The modern Dip was introduced by descendants of the aforementioned Joseph Goddard. It comes in a wide-mouthed jar, and any object too large for immersion in it can have the liquid applied with a soft brush or a pad of cotton-wool. In both instances application of the solution should be for no longer than is necessary, and the article should then be washed thoroughly. A gentle rubbing after it has dried is the final requirement.

Foam

This is applied all over the article with a dampened sponge. It forms a lather, and after a short time it can be washed off together with dirt and tarnish. Again, after drying, rubbing is necessary.

With all the above methods it will be seen that a certain amount of rubbing is required in order to achieve a good shine.

Alternatively, polishing can be done with an impregnated cotton cloth, with a liquid polish, or with an impregnated wadding. All of them remove some of the silver surface and in so doing are liable to dirty the hands. These are best protected with thin cotton gloves that will not harm the articles being held.

Care should be taken not to rub the marks more than necessary or they will eventually become illegible. If they do, some of the history of the article is lost, and at the same time it is worth less on the market.

Salt-cellars should be given special attention, as salt will attack the metal and finally eat holes in it. A glass liner should be removed regularly to ensure that no grains have slipped between it and the salt-cellar.

Silver that is to be stored or is used only occasionally should be polished, wrapped in acid-free tissue-paper, and put into polythene or baize bags, or into specially-treated bags made and marketed for the purpose.

Finally, silver-gilt has to be treated with extra care to make certain that the coating of gold is not scratched or otherwise damaged. Polishing is not recommended. Warm water and a little soap are the best answer, followed by careful drying. Silver-gilt should be kept in a dry place, away from damp.

Pair of wine coolers by Benjamin and James Smith, 1810. Silver-gilt, height 33 cm. *Christie's.* The shape and decoration were inspired by Classical originals

TABLES OF WEIGHTS

Troy
1 pound equals 12 oz
1 oz equals 20 dwt
1 dwt equals 24 grains

Avoirdupois
1 pound equals 16 oz
1 oz equals 16 drams

Troy ounces to Avoirdupois
Multiply Troy oz by 1.0971

Avoirdupois ounces to Troy
Multiply Avoirdupois oz by 0.09115

Troy to Metric grammes
1 dwt equals 1.555 grammes
5 dwt equals 7.775 grammes
10 dwt equals 15.551 grammes
15 dwt equals 23.327 grammes
1 oz equals 31.103 grammes
12 oz equals 373.242 grammes

Troy to Metric
Troy oz to grammes, multiply oz by 31.1035
Avoirdupois oz to grammes, multiply by 28.3495

Glossary of Terms

Acanthus A plant common in the Mediterranean area, recognised by its shiny and deeply serrated leaves. It became popular in western Europe as a decorative feature during the renaissance.

Alloy A mixture of two or more metals. Silver alloyed with copper acquires durability.

Annealing To heat and then cool metal when hammering it avoids brittleness and splitting that would otherwise occur.

Anthemion A classical ornament resembling the flower of the honeysuckle favoured by Robert Adam and his followers.

Arabesque Ornament characterised by scrolling foliage interspersed with human figures, birds, and so forth.

Astragal A small half-round moulding.

Auricular Ornament of swirling cartilaginous forms that bear a resemblance to the human ear.

Baluster A pillar or column bulging towards the base; when reversed it is known as an inverted baluster.

Beading Ornament in the form of closely-placed half-pearls.

Branch Two or more candle-holders on an arm that can be fitted to a candlestick and convert it into a candelabra. Also, once used to describe a chandelier.

Bright-cut Decoration in the form of shining facets.

Britannia standard The quality of silver mandatory between 1697 and 1720 and thereafter obligatory. It is composed of 10 dwt of copper in each 1 lb Troy of pure silver, or 985 parts of the latter in 1000.

Cartouche An ornamental surround for a coat of arms, inscription etc derived from a partially-unrolled scroll of paper or parchment.

Casting Articles and parts of articles formed by pouring the molten metal into a mould and then removing blemishes. See *Lost wax*.

Chasing Decoration in relief achieved by hammering the metal with punches without removing any of it. See *Flat chasing, Repoussé*.

Chinoiserie A European version of an Oriental pattern.

Cut-card A shaped and pierced sheet of silver soldered to the body of an article, such as the base of a bowl or the junction of a handle, providing decoration as well as reinforcement.

Date Letter A letter of the alphabet selected by the Goldsmiths' Company to denote the year of assay.

Engraving To ornament by cutting into the metal with a graver to make patterns composed of fine lines and dots. Used also for armorials, initials and other signs of ownership, as well as inscriptions.

Feather Edge A border of wedge-like facets giving a resemblance to its name.

Filigree Openwork ornament formed from silver wire and beads soldered into scrolling patterns.

Flat Chasing Chasing in low relief sometimes used in conjunction with engraving, with which it can be confused.

Fluting Parallel half-round channels.

Gadroon A series of radiating short lobes forming a border.

Hall Mark The series of marks stamped on silverware that testifies to the purity of the metal, gives the date and place of assay, where appropriate if duty on it has been paid, and the maker's name.

Imbrication A scale-pattern of overlapping shapes in the manner of a tiled roof.

Lost Wax A casting process using a wax model enclosed in a fireproof casing. The wax melting as molten silver is poured in.

Mask Term for a head, male or female, human or otherwise, used as a decorative motif.

Mantling Decoration about a coat of arms taking the form of plumes, foliage or drapery.

Parcel-gilt Partly gilt.

Patera A circular or oval disc usually with a central raised boss from which radiate stylised leaves.

Planish To produce a smooth surface by removing traces of the hammer blows gained during manufacture.

Pricked Work Initials, dates and decoration engraved in a series of small dots resembling pin-pricks.

Rat Tail A tapering ridge found under the bowl of a spoon where it joins the stem.

Reeding Parallel raised moulded ribs that resemble stalks of reeds and are the reverse of fluting.

Repoussé Relief patterns worked up from the back and usually finished with chasing.

Rococo Ornament comprising rock and shell forms and other detail derived from grottoes arranged with scrolls in an asymmetrical manner.

Sheffield Plate A method of covering a piece of copper with one of silver and fusing them together was devised by a Sheffield cutler, Thomas Boulsover, in about 1742; double-plating, with copper sandwiched between two pieces of silver, came into use in the late 1760s.

Sterling standard Composed of 18 dwt of copper to each 11 oz 2 dwt of pure silver or 925 parts of the latter in 1000.

Strapwork Ribbon-like bands or straps forming a pattern.

Swag A festoon or garland of flowers, fruit or drapery fixed at either end and hanging down in the middle.

Thumbpiece The raised member above the hinge of a lid by which the latter can be raised by thumb-pressure.

Tine The prong or spike of a fork.

Touch To test the purity of silver by use of a touchstone, to mark an article after so testing, and the mark itself.

Trefid a three-lobed terminal on a spoon or on the feet of other articles.

Wrigglework An engraved zig-zag line.

List of Sources

Judith Banister, *Collecting Antique Silver*, 1972

Elaine Barr, *George Wickes*, 1980

Elisabeth Bennion, *Antique Medical Instruments*, 1979

Roger M. Berkowitz, 'The Patriotic Fund Vases' in APOLLO, Vol. CXIII, No. 228 (February 1981)

Frederick Bradbury (Ed.), *British Assay Office Marks*, Sheffield

Joseph Brasbridge, *The Fruits of Experience*, 2nd. edn., 1824

Thomas Campbell, *Diary of a visit to England in 1775* (Ed. J. C. Clifford), Cambridge, 1947

Richard Carew *Survey of Cornwall*, 1602

Michael Clayton, *The Collector's Dictionary of the Silver and Gold of Great Britain and North America*, 1971

A. J. Collins, *Inventory of the Jewels and Plate of Queen Elizabeth I*, 1955

J. Charles Cox and Alfred Harvey, *English Church Furniture*, 1907

John Culme, *Nineteenth-Century Silver*, 1977

John D. Davis, *English Silver at Williamsburg*, Colonial Williamsburg, Va., 1976

H. W. Dickinson, *Matthew Boulton*, Cambridge, 1937

John Evelyn, *Diary* (Ed. E. S. de Beer), six vols., 1955

J. P. Fallon, *The Marks of the London Goldsmiths (c. 1697–1837)*, Newton Abbot, 1972

Celia Fiennes, *Through England on a Side Saddle*, 1888; reprinted as *The Journeys of Celia Fiennes* (Ed. C. Morris), 1949

Gentleman's Magazine, 1731 etc

Arthur G. Grimwade, *London Goldsmiths 1697–1837*, 1976, revised edn. 1982

William Harrison, *Description of England*, printed in R. Holinshed's *Chronicles of England*, 1577, revised 1587

J. F. Hayward, *Huguenot Silver in England 1688–1727*, 1959

Ambrose Heal, *London Goldsmiths 1200–1800*, 1935

John Hervey, first Earl of Bristol, *Diary* (Ed. S.H.A.H.), Wells, 1894

Sir C. J. Jackson, *English Goldsmiths and Their Marks*, 2nd. edn., 1921, reprinted 1949 and subsequently

William Kitchiner, *The Cook's Oracle*, new edition, 1829

R. W. Lightbown, 'Christian van Vianen' in APOLLO, Vol. XXXVII, No. 76 (June 1968)

Daniel and Samuel Lysons, *Magna Britannia, III: Cornwall*, 1814

Georgina E. Lee, *British Silver Monteith Bowls*, 1978

Elizabeth B. Miles, *The English Silver Pocket Nutmeg Grater*, privately published, 1966

John S. Moore (Ed.), *The Goods and Chattels of our Forefathers*, 1976

W. M. Myddelton (Ed.), *Chirk Castle Accounts 1666–1753*, Manchester, 1931

J. E. Nightingale, *Church Plate of the County of Wilts.*, Salisbury, 1891

Charles Oman, *English Domestic Silver*, 7th edn., 1968; *English Church Plate*, 1957; *The English Silver in the Kremlin*, 1961; *Caroline Silver 1625–88*, 1970; *English Engraved Silver 1150–1900*, 1978

N. M. Penzer, *The Book of the Wine-Label*, 1947; *Paul Storr*, 1954; 'What is a Mazarine?' in APOLLO, Vol. LXI, No. 362 (April 1955)

Samuel Pepys, *Diary* (Ed. R. C. Latham and W. Matthews), 1970–83

Sophie von la Roche, *Sophie in London, 1786* (Trans. Clare Williams, 1933

Robert Rowe, *Adam Silver*, 1965

Arthur Ryland, *The Assay of Gold and Silver Wares*, 1852

J. T. Smith, *A Book for a Rainy Day*, 1845

Gladys Scott Thomson, *The Russells in Bloomsbury 1669–1771*, 1940

Peter Thornton and Maurice Tomlin, *The Furnishing and Decoration of Ham House*, 1980

Kurt Ticher, Ida Delamer and William O'Sullivan, *Hall Marks on Dublin Silver 1730–72*, Dublin, 1978

G. M. Trevelyan, *English Social History*, 3rd. edn., 1946

Victoria and Albert Museum, *English Church Art* (Exhibition catalogue), 1971

Patricia Wardle, *Victorian Silver and Silver-Plate*, 1963

Thomas Westcote, *View of Devonshire in MDCXXX*, Exeter, 1845

Hamil Westwood, 'A Touchstone . . . the Author W. B. identified' in APOLLO, Vol. LXXL, No. 423 (May 1960)

Wynyard R. T. Wilkinson, *A History of Hallmarks*, revised edn., 1975

Sir Henry Trueman Wood, *History of the Royal Society of Arts*, 1913

General Index

References in bold type are to colour plates, and those in *italic* are to black and white illustrations.

INDEX OF SILVERSMITHS

Index compiled by Audrey Bamber